MY CAPITOL SECRETS

For five glamorous years Rita Jenrette lived the way most women dream. As a Congressman's wife, life was an endless party in the fish bowl of a dazzling social and political world. Then, on October 7, 1980, everything changed.

Her estranged husband, former Representative John Jenrette, a Democrat from the 6th District in South Carolina, was convicted on charges of bribery and conspiracy in the notorious FBI Abscam case.

Now Rita has decided to spill the supershocking secrets of her life—and life in our nation's capitol.

RITA JENRETTE
MY CAPITOL SECRETS

BANTAM BOOKS
TORONTO · NEW YORK · LONDON · SYDNEY

MY CAPITOL SECRETS
A Bantam Book / March 1981

ISBN 0–553–20190–2

Published simultaneously in the United States and Canada

Bantam Books are published by Bantam Books, Inc. Its trade-
mark, consisting of the words "Bantam Books" and the por-
trayal of a bantam, is Registered in U.S. Patent and Trademark
Office and in other countries. Marca Registrada. Bantam
Books, Inc., 666 Fifth Avenue, New York, New York 10103.

PRINTED IN THE UNITED STATES OF AMERICA

0 9 8 7 6 5 4 3 2 1

This book is dedicated to my parents,
Reba and C.H. Carpenter,
whose love is always there

ACKNOWLEDGMENTS

Gladys Brown, Stacey Brown, Ginger and Brad Brown, Jim Abourezk, Julie Babinas, Paul Bricker, Wanda Lee and Winston Brown, J.B. Caddaro, Mark Carliner. Marvin Chernoff, Oleg Chichilnitsky, Gayle Cohen, Jeff Cohen, Mrs. Van Dooser, May Garlington, Cathy Gattuso, Tim Graham, Marilyn Grabowski, Christine Green, Milton Greene, Cynthia Hayashi, Hugh Hefner, Wayne Herndon, Ray Hoehle, Judith Jordan, Julietta, Ann Loew, Anthony Loew, Linda LoPresti, Janet Love, Claire Lyons, Kathy Maxa, Rudy Maxa, Louise McClure, Dr. Phil Moser, Jeanie Musselman, Allen Nixon, Leonard Nixon, Elizabeth Norris, Pompeo Posar, Sam Pryor, Blanche Ricks, Donna Rogers, Bob Rose, Stanley Rothenberg, Maggie Falvey, Elin Schoen, Dr. Claudio Segre, Gene Stone, Dick and Germaine Swanson, Louise Timm, Dr. Herbert Woodbury.

Contents

Prologue

Saturday, February 2, 1980, was one of those perfect, golden winter days. I lay on the raw-silk sofa in the living room of the three-story home that my husband and I had been furnishing since the early days of our marriage—a small house, by Washington politicians' standards, within walking distance from the Hill. The decor was truly a team effort, a labor of love. John had supplied many of the antique pieces; my mother had sent my family-heirloom silver from Texas. There were objects John and I had chosen together in Kuala Lumpur, Peking, London, on trips connected with John's position as congressional representative of the 6th district of South Carolina and on personal trips, attempts to get away from the pressures of the Hill and spend time alone in our unofficial capacity as Mr. and Mrs. Jenrette.

This particular weekend, I thought, would be as solitary as if we had flown to some remote corner of the world. John, who had just returned from his customary weekly trip to South Carolina, lolled on the loveseat across from me, his tie loosened, his shirt rumpled. The sunlight flooded through the two *grand windows behind him. He had been drinking on the flight from Myrtle Beach. Airline personnel, upon recognizing congressmen or senators traveling economy, customarily upgrade them to first class where they can have all the free drinks they want. John had thoroughly availed himself of Eastern's generosity; he was flushed, a little too jovial, but he had never looked so handsome. He seemed to share my happiness at having two days, finally, to ourselves. After so many months of never a private moment, the crises that had helped keep us apart were over.*

"We've weathered everything, I thought. We're going to be okay. John had just been cleared of charges of drug smuggling, jury tampering, and selling underwater lots. We were home free. I sipped my Diet Dr. Pepper and looked around the living room, which seemed to embody everything good in our life together. We had bought the ancient blue and brown silk carpet in New Delhi. On the delicate French table next to the sofa was a framed photograph of John and me on Air Force One, with President Carter shaking my hand. The picture was signed, "To Rita and John, with warmest regards, Jimmy." Another cherished photograph, of John and me shivering in front of the emperor's palace in Tokyo, stood on an antique desk. We had filled the miniature breakfront next to the beautiful wooden staircase with Royal Copenhagen figurines, a Japanese saki set, plates from China, primitive objects given to us by the aborigines we visited in the forests of New Guinea—against the better judgment of our driver—a hand-carved whistle, a fertility statue, and water vases made of mud and saliva. On a Louis XIV table—used, I enjoyed telling visitors, by courtiers for the disposal of bones during

2

meals—was a silver plate engraved "To Rita and John with warmest regards, Nancy and Strom Thurmond, 9/10/76"—a wedding gift.

I ignored the first, faint, ringing sounds. The doorbell was broken. Whoever was outside didn't know this. Eventually they might give up and go away. Or maybe it was just my imagination, paranoia from years of interrupted intimacy. But the tiny sound persisted. Then there was loud knocking on the door. "John," I said, "did you forget to tell me that some constituent of yours was coming to visit?" It was not an improbability.

John's "friends" from South Carolina, often people we had met only once over cocktails, showed up at our house with annoying frequency, sometimes just to say "hi" to their congressman, sometimes with oddball requests—such as the man who, upon his arrival in Washington, rushed right over to our place and asked if he could take a shower. I had never met him before. (John told him to come right on in.) Then there was the mother and daughter who spent a weekend at a Washington hotel. John picked up the $400 tab; I took them to lunch and showed them the sights. John's Southern hospitality tended to get out of hand. "Come up to Washington and see us," he'd tell total strangers who until that moment had expected nothing from him except a handshake.

But he knew nothing, he assured me, about whoever was banging on our front door that Saturday afternoon. "This is our weekend," he said.

"Well, whoever it is, I'm telling them you're not here." I assumed that the intrusion concerned him. Who would want to see me? I was just John Jenrette's wife. I had long since lost any sense of the former Rita Carpenter.

3

I walked reluctantly to the door and pulled back the shirred curtain and looked outside. Two men in trenchcoats stood on the porch. They had very short hair. Each of them carried a black briefcase. They didn't look like constituents.

I opened the door a crack. "Yes?"

"Is Congressman Jenrette at home?" one of the men asked.

"No, he's not."

"Ma'am, we'd really like to talk to him."

John interrupted: "Let 'em come in."

The two men strode into the foyer. John rose to greet them. They showed him their FBI identification cards. John asked them to sit down.

Just then, the phone began ringing in the kitchen, our private line. No one except selected members of John's staff knew the number. What now? I thought as I ran into the kitchen and picked up the phone. It was Richard Davis, John's right-hand political man. "Rita," he said, "I've gotta talk to John." The panic in his voice alarmed me. I told Richard that John couldn't come to the phone. "Oh, God," Richard said, "I'm in a phone booth. A New York Times reporter just called me." And Richard went on to tell me all about Abscam.

"What in the world is Abscam?" I asked.

"It's some sort of bribe thing. They think John took a bribe. Some Arabs were involved. The Times has the whole story."

I walked back into the living room, dazed, just as one of the FBI agents asked John whether he knew "a guy named Tony DeVito." I saw John's face go white. I felt sick. Both phones were ringing now. Members of the press. Members of John's staff. The FBI questions were coming faster, followed by John's denials, until—"Mr. Jenrette," one of the men said gruffly, "we've got you on videotape."

4

I felt as if my head were about to explode. "How dare you set up my husband?" I screamed, rushing up to the two intruders. "He's innocent! You set him up on that drug thing, the underwater-lot thing. Now you've finally got him. Are you proud of yourselves?"

The two men stood up, too shocked to say anything. I kept at them. "I want you to write down your home addresses," I yelled, "and your home phone numbers. You know where we live. You know our phone number. I think we deserve to know where you live."

"We can only give you our office number, ma'am."

"I want your home numbers."

By this time, John had recovered his equilibrium. He demanded that the two men give him back the release form he had signed when they first walked in the door. They refused. John started yelling. "Give me that fucking form." The agents had put on their coats and were backing out the door. John followed them, still shouting, "Don't you ever come back here again."

Our lawyers soon arrived; reporters from all three networks and every major newspaper were starting to camp outside our house. We kept the blinds drawn and the curtains closed. When I called Bob and Linda in New York late that night, I couldn't stop crying. Bob and Linda had been my closest friends for almost as long as I had been married to John. They had helped me through some awful times, but what had just happened and what was to come were worse than anything we could have imagined. "They got him," I sobbed into the phone. "They got him."

That night, the cameras were set up outside my house, ready to roll. I was used to facing the press already. John and I had made People magazine even in the early stages of our romance. But I didn't feel like a celebrity. I felt like a prisoner. Come to think of it, I had felt like a prisoner ever since I married John Jenrette.

One
Welcome
to Washington

The ballroom in the Capitol Hilton was crowded and
noisy. There was a sparkle of jewels in the chandelier light, shrieks of laughter over the general hub-
bub, ice clacking in shot glasses. It was one of those
Washington events known generically as a political
function. It could have been cocktails and dinner
hosted by a trucking association or a power company
—electricity and gas, that is, because all of the
capital party givers represent power one way or the
other. Or our hosts could have been a state travel
association or a state university or a manufacturer
of just about anything or any group from any state
with a product or a purpose. I don't remember whose
party it was, just the general impression of one of
those endless social gatherings where you greet and
chat with hundreds of the same people you saw at
the last endless social gathering.

But I remember that this particular event took
place shortly after John and I got married, so it
must have been at the end of September 1976. And I
remember running into Lindy Boggs. Lindy was one
of my favorite people in Washington. She was the
widow of Hale Boggs, the Louisiana congressman,

who was one of the prime movers of the House of Representatives at the time of his death in a plane crash in Alaska in 1974. Lindy had been elected to fill his seat in the House. She knew Washington from a very unique double prespective: she had seen it as a congressman's wife, and then she saw it as a congressperson herself.

Lindy smiled at John and me. "You're married now!" she said.

I nodded. Word had gotten around town fast, but then it always did.

"You have my sincerest sympathy," Lindy said, suddenly serious. "Both of you."

I was stunned speechless. I had always admired Lindy so much. She was one of the strongest, most intelligent women I'd ever met. As we walked away, I looked at John. "She doesn't like us!" I said.

Four years later, John and I attended virtually the same political function in the ballroom of the Capitol Hilton. When I saw Lindy Boggs, I experienced a feeling of déjà vu. This time, however, I spoke to her first. "Lindy," I said, "I know what you mean now."

I never will forget the first time I saw John Wilson Jenrette, Jr. It was my first day in Washington, in the summer of 1975. I stood on the steps of the Longworth House Office building debating which route to take to the Republican National Committee's (RNC) Eisenhower Building. I felt a hand touch my arm. The man standing next to me was wearing the loudest jacket I had ever seen: green, orange, and gold plaid. I had just walked past him inside the building, and our eyes had met briefly.

But the unbelievably gaudy jacket was the reason I remembered him. Whatever we said to each other initially was unmemorable—the usual pleasantries, I suppose, banalities about the sweltering weather. But it soon became apparent that this man's manner was as bold as his jacket. He told me that he was an elevator operator in the Capitol. This seemed plausible. Being an elevator operator on the Hill is one of the best jobs a political up-and-comer can have, and this man looked as if he were in his early thirties (although he was, as it turned out, thirty-nine).

I had been a Capitol Hill elevator operator myself about a year before during a previous, brief flirtation with living in Washington. It was one of the best jobs in D.C., I thought—good pay, short hours, and virtually a crash course in political wheeling and dealing for those who know how to keep their ears open and their mouths shut. More political business is conducted on those elevators than one could imagine. You learn who is in and who is out, who the big players are, and which men and women are just bit players. And the elevator operators are not merely privy to political intrigue; a lot of extracongressional goings-on also enter into elevator banter. And whether the eavesdropper at the elevator controls is hearing truth or fiction about the social life of this legislator or that lobbyist, the talk is fun to hear.

There was something about John Jenrette that fascinated me despite his unfortunate taste in jackets. He seemed to be either the most charming man I had ever met or the kind of man your mother always told you to avoid! As we strolled toward the Capitol, I asked myself why I was gravitating toward the direction he was taking. (I had my own plans for the afternoon.) John was making some fairly outrageous suggestions that just didn't jibe with his Southern-boy drawl and his innocent blue eyes. Would I like to take off to the Virgin Islands with him? We could sunbathe together in the nude, he thought.

Then, perhaps sensing that his line of chatter had gone beyond the bounds of good judgment, he toned it down. We entered the Capitol Building, and I was surprised when he guided me toward the "Members Only" elevator. I thought, *Either this guy has an awful lot of pull for an elevator operator, or he's totally brazen and foolhardy.*

Then, the so-called elevator operator pushed through another "Members Only" door on to the floor of the House of Representatives and into the action as if he were really a part of it—which, I suddenly realized, he was. I must have been looking absolutely dumbstruck because when he saw the look on my face, he burst out laughing. I liked his hearty laugh, although I still didn't know what to make of him.

As I soon found out, John Jenrette, of South Carolina was one of the new breed of congressmen who had been elected during the Watergate backlash. The 94th Congress was young and idealistic, a new breed out to change the world—or the legislative system, at the very least. And John was truly at the head of the class, so to speak: he had been elected freshman Whip. In this position, he quickly used his charm and ability to maneuver himself a position of considerable influence—so much so that the *Washington Post*, in covering a D.C. Cong. Walter E. Fauntroy political function, would cite John as one of the most powerful political movers in Congress. And John Jenrette would be one of the congressmen Tip O'Neill would name in a TV interview as a possible successor to him as speaker of the House.

I walked with John to his congressional office where his staff greeted me with all the warmth they would have displayed had John just arrived with an army of computers and announced, "This is my new staff. You're all fired."

In retrospect, I suppose I can understand the frosty reception, although at the time I couldn't imagine what I had done to deserve it. I didn't know John socially, of course, any more than I knew his political track record. As it turned out, he was not only a mover in the House of Representatives. I suppose the best way to describe him in those days would be as one of Washington's most eligible bachelors, although he was divorced. His two teen-age children lived with his first wife in his home town of North Myrtle Beach, South Carolina. John lived alone in a townhouse a few blocks from the Capitol building, but he was far from lonely. If his staffers took a look at me that day and sighed inwardly and thought, *Oh, another girl friend,* the assumption was not unfounded.

John introduced me to his administrative assistant, John F. Clark III, who started questioning me about my employment references. It seemed that Clark had been told to find a position on the staff for Rita Carpenter, although I hadn't asked for a job. In fact, I was in Washington that summer to accept an offer as opposition research director of the RNC. And that's what I told Clark.

"I didn't ask for a job," I said, and I got up to leave.

"Oh, don't leave now," John said. "Where are you staying?"

"At the Shoreham Americana."

I had a date that night with Bob O'Dell, who is now a Reagan fundraiser. I was getting dressed to go out when the first call from John Jenrette came. I told him that I had a date. He said, "Well, get rid of him. And I'll get rid of my date."

"No," I told him. The suggestion convinced me that not only did I not want to see John Jenrette that night, I didn't want to go out with him at all. The idea of being in the position of whoever was his date that night didn't appeal to me. And if he'd stand her up because he'd just met someone he thought he preferred, undoubtedly he'd be just as quick to stand me up for someone new.

That night, after I returned from my date, the phone kept ringing until around four in the morning —always John Jenrette, begging me to go out with him. And I kept refusing. I told myself that I didn't like him. Furthermore, I told myself, I had big plans for my future in Washington. I was going to be a serious career woman. I was not going to get drawn into the local social whirl. No man was going to distract me from my career objectives, not even a congressman.

But Congressman Jenrette had certainly made an impression on me. His extraordinary interest was flattering, intriguing, and surprising, for somewhere inside me I was still the awkward Rita Carpenter whom nobody at Lamar Junior High School in Austin, Texas, seemed to like. Nothing could dissuade me from the profound conviction that anyone who paid me a compliment was either blind or a liar. After I had started dating John Jenrette, the same *Washington Post* item that described him as a powerful political mover also mentioned that he had been observed with a blonde on his arm who would turn "ah" into a five-syllable word. My immediate reaction was "What blonde? Who else has he been seeing?" Then I realized that the columnist meant me. I was grateful, as if I were back in seventh grade and had gotten some unexpected praise or attention from my peers, which I never did.

Actually, my classmates weren't my peers. When

I was in kindergarten in San Antonio, I was put ahead two grades. My parents then moved from San Antonio to Austin, Texas, when I was ten. Our house in San Antonio had been beautiful—horseshoe shaped, with a swimming pool landscaped with banana and gardenia trees. I had what has been described as a "pampered" childhood. I suppose it was in that I felt comfortable at home and my parents and I were close.

But at school things were not so comfortable. While the girls in my class were thirteen years old and developing figures and wearing makeup, I was a frumpy eleven-year-old who wore glasses. And I hadn't grown up with these kids; I was fresh from San Antonio. So nobody knew me very well; and they didn't try to get to know me. They simply called me "four eyes." One time, I overcame my shyness and asked one of the girls, Linda Pavhlis, if I could eat lunch with her. She always had lunch with two of the cutest cheerleaders, twins named Mary and Ann Byers. Linda and I were standing at the top of the gym stairs. So she walked to the bottom of the stairs and asked Mary and Ann, "Can Rita Carpenter eat with us?"

And I heard the answer, "Oh, no. She's ugly."

Every day I took my lunch into the gym bathroom and ate with my feet up on the door so the monitor couldn't see that I was in there.

I stayed reclusive and scared until the age of fourteen when suddenly boys who had never given me a second look were now staring at me. Suddenly, I was being asked to go to parties and join clubs. I went to two high schools, and at both of them I ran for offices and entered contests—beauty contests, popularity contests, whatever—with a vengeance, all to make up, I think, for those years of being ignored. I was a cheerleader, "Football Sweetheart,"

"Senior Class Favorite," prom queen, star of my senior-class musical *On with the Show,* photojournalist for the senior newspaper, officer on the student council. Every Sunday I did volunteer work at the Travis State School for the Retarded, and I tutored high school students and some dropouts in Montopolis, the Chicano section of Austin. I had one boy friend all through high school, Tim Graham, tall, thin, with the bluest-blue eyes and blond hair. I never dated anyone else. I probably should have married him.

But college broke up what was, trite though it sounds, the love of my life. I went to four colleges. I would have been happy to stay at the first one, St. Edwards University, but my parents literally yanked me out of the school after I converted to Catholicism. (I had fallen in love with a Dominican priest and had decided to become a nun. My devout Methodist parents arrived at St. Edwards at midnight one night and took me—and my car—back home.)

Oklahoma State University, the next stop in my education, seemed like the end of the earth. I reverted back to my old reclusive behavior, doing anything to avoid classes. If there was ice on the road, I would fall down in order not to have to go to class. After one semester of misery, I transferred to Monticello College, a very conservative, religiously-affiliated girl's school near Alton, Illinois, where I met a man who affected my life more than anyone had before. He was my English professor, Herbert Woodbury. He seemed to take me more seriously than my grades warranted. I spent little time studying. This was 1968; I was busy protesting.

One Sunday, at the school's weekly church service, I gave a speech called "The Angry Youth" and really blasted the president of the college. Dr. Woodbury took me aside after the service and said, "Rita, someday I think you're going to do something that will really help people in this life and in this world. You're a very special person. But you're not going to accomplish anything for yourself or for anyone else by rebelling and getting into trouble and not studying and not going to class."

By the time I graduated, a few years later, from the University of Texas, I was an honors student. I was also engaged to be married. My parents were relieved when I brought Skip Ward home to meet them. All the young men I had brought home previously had had long hair and wire-rimmed glasses and tended to major in protesting and getting tear gassed by the Texas Rangers during various demonstrations. Skip, an all-American football player who had presented me with a gigantic diamond engagement ring, was different. And I thought, *Well, why not get married?* I was graduating from college. What else could I do? I had applied to the Peace Corps, but marrying Skip seemed the more sensible alternative.

It was going to be a big wedding. The preparations seemed endless, from choosing the right dress for me to making sure each bridesmaid was happy with her dress to selecting, addressing, and sending out the invitations. Two weeks before the ceremony, the Peace Corps informed me that my application had been accepted. And I admitted to myself—I had been fighting the feeling—that I didn't love Skip the way a woman should love the man who will be her husband. I returned the gigantic diamond to Skip and left for Papaikou, Hawaii, to train for six years in Micronesia. But my Peace Corps career ended after only two weeks of getting up at five A.M. and sleeping with clothes and blankets on top of me in tropical heat because I was afraid of the unrecognizable insects and cat-sized rats lurking in the sugar-cane field where we were camped out. I couldn't take it. I went back to Austin, to become a singer. Since I was obviously not cut out for saving the world, I decided to try to entertain it.

My singing career took off immediately. I was offered a recording contract with a company in Dallas. Naturally, I wanted to accept; this was going to be easier than I thought. Obviously, I was a real talent. With visions of Grace Slick dancing in my head, I went to the office of the man who was going to make me a star.

"Well, now," he drawled, "if ah asked you to drive a car and you had never driven one before, what would you do?"

I thought about this for a minute and then told him, "I'd probably go ahead and drive the car because that's the way I am, you know."

"Ah see," he said, "Well, now. Will you do everything ah ask you to do without question?"

This time I spoke without thinking about it. "Yes." After all, he was the one who knew the record business. I was merely there to be marketed. Just like in the movies.

"Well, now," he said. "Ah'd like you to take off your clothes."

This wasn't in the script I had in mind. I took off my right shoe and waited. He waited, too, his eyes bright with anticipation.

I put the shoe back on. "That's it," I said, walking over to him. "You're going to be sorry you ever asked me to do this," I said. "I'm going to be a big star someday. And you're going to regret asking me to do this."

I sailed to the door, preparing to yank it open and make my dramatic exit, ending my big scene with a bang. The door was stuck. My big scene whimpered to a close. So, for the time being, did my recording plans.

Then, when I met Rick Coleman, a dashingly handsome pilot who drove a Morgan, I fell for him immediately. But the romance was not as rosy as I thought. Rick, it turned out, was overly susceptible to the many women who pursued him. I decided, more to "show him" than to pursue any particular career, that I would move to Washington, D.C.

I happened to have one friend in Washington; we had been at Monticello together. I moved in with her, both of us with no furniture, just two mattresses on the floor. I then came by my first job accidentally. One of the architects of the Capitol was having lunch several tables from mine in the Capitol cafeteria. He asked me if I wanted a job.

"What kind of job?" Although most people would be suspicious of a stranger who suddenly offered them a job while they were eating a tuna fish salad sandwich in the lunchroom of our nation's leading office building, I was merely curious.

"Come by my office," he said.

When the architect told me that the opening he had was for an elevator operator, I was somewhat disappointed. After having served notice to everyone I knew in Austin that they could expect "Rita Carpenter Goes to Washington" to be the start of something big (at this point in my life, I was heavily influenced by movies with Horatio Alger overtones), how could I write home and say I'd found gainful employment as an elevator operator? But I changed my mind when I found out that the job of elevator operator is one of the most coveted on the Hill.

To be sure, the work was not exactly challenging. But I learned a lot. One thing I learned was that I'd have to be a bit more discriminating about who I took up on offers to "drop by my office." One day, I was approached by the late Arthus Dennis Devouard "Dev" O'Neill, who was then the Democrats' official photographer. (The Republicans, too, have a photographer at the Capitol to take photos of legislators for publicity or personal use at no charge.) Dev thought I had the potential to become a model. I thought, *Oh, well, he's getting on in years.* But on the off chance that he wasn't senile, it really would be deeply satisfying, I reasoned, to know that Mary and Ann Byers were eating their hearts out over my picture on the cover of *Vogue.* I met O'Neill in his office as he had requested. He did, indeed, take many photographs of me, some with a Bozo the Clown robot that was to be used at the 1972 Democratic National Convention. And then, while adjusting the collar of my jacket, he suddenly slipped his hand inside my blouse.

If I had thought that my reporting this lecher to the architect of the Capitol might have cost him his job, I would have done so. But it seemed pointless. Dev O'Neill was a congressional legend, brought in by Sam Rayburn himself. Therefore, Dev O'Neill had more clout than Rita Carpenter, neophyte elevator operator. If anything, a complaint might cost me my job. I may have been—and may still be—naive, but even then I knew that, especially in male-chauvinist Washington, women who accuse well-connected and powerful men of less-than-gentlemanly behavior are more likely to cause trouble for themselves than the men. An incident such as Dev O'Neill's fumble could easily be misconstrued, making him look innocent and me like a seductress. In fact, just my going to his office and remaining there alone with him was suspect. Everyone knows that many Capitol offices are not for business only.

I never told anyone what Dev O'Neill had done.

After a few months as an elevator operator, I went to work with the Advisory Commission on Intergovernmental Relations, a presidential commission on, not surprisingly, intergovernmental relations. But my coworkers and I didn't hit it off. And I missed Rick, the dashing pilot I had left behind in Austin. I called him. He said, "Come back home. We'll get married." So I did what I had been conditioned to do, after all. I deserted Washington for Rick.

The marriage lasted for about a year. We were just totally wrong for each other. I think that the only reason the relationship lasted as long as it did was that Rick was the only man I had ever made love with. And I was brought up to believe that when you get married, that's it for life and that sex with anyone other than your husband is a sin.

I still believe that to this day.

So although it was clear almost from the outset that my marriage with Rick was a failure, it took me a while to face up to the fact that what I thought would be forever had, in fact, been a mistake.

During my marriage my career plans—I should say, my plans to be somebody since I had no clearer picture now of what exactly my career would be than I had in college—were in limbo. For a while, I sold Elizabeth Arden cosmetics at Scarbrough's Department Store in Austin.

Then, through an employment agency, I landed a job with Jim Granberry, the Republican Candidate for governor in 1974. My only political experience had been as a campaign worker for then senator Ralph Yarborough when I was a student at the University of Texas. But I had minored in political science at school, and I had always been politically involved, although my philosophy did not make me an ideal candidate for employment by the Republicans.

Jim Granberry's Democratic opponent was conservative Dolph Briscoe. So I rationalized that even though I was a liberal—a bleeding-heart liberal, in fact, and I still am, and I'm proud of it—somehow being a Republican in Texas and working against Dolph Briscoe was more liberal than being a "Yellow Dog Democrat."

Within a few months, I became research director of the Republican party of Texas. But I left the job at around the same time I shocked Rick with the news that I was leaving him. I announced my intentions to him one night, just like that. "I'm leaving." He was incredulous, as I knew he would be and as he really shouldn't have been; my unhappiness was obvious even to casual friends. We were mismatched. Rick, like all too many men, I've learned, never really listened to what his wife was trying to tell him until it was too late. He never communicated. Finally, there was nothing left to say, anyway, except good-by.

I was twenty-five years old when I moved to Washington, D.C.—again. But this time, a job was waiting as "opposition research director" of the RNC. That meant that I would work, with my staff of thirteen, to scrounge up information that could be used to undermine the campaigns and, in the long run, the political careers of certain Democratic incumbents. I had gotten the job through my research work with the Republican party of Texas after having spent a year in Paris purging myself of marital memories. Although I wasn't particularly enamored of what my job entailed, I had been told, "Work very hard and we'll get Jerry Ford reelected, and you'll end up at the White House." Anyway, I was also told, the Democrats were doing the same thing. That's the way politics is and always has been. If you can't play rough, you might as well find yourself a tamer game. But if the raison d'être of my job was something I'd like to forget, the work, from day to day, was intriguing in the same way reading gossip columns is. In fact, we read a lot of gossip columns, newspapers from all over the country, clipping tidbits to file in the computerized dossiers the RNC was compiling on such legislators as Hubert Humphrey, George McGovern, Birch Bayh, Frank Church, John Tunney, John Culver, and Tip O'Neill. And the RNC did more blatant detective work than that. My first assignment, in fact, was to get on a plane and go to Worcester, Massachusetts, armed with a fake press pass, and dig up dirt on Sen. John Durkin of New Hampshire. My instructions were to go to the *Boston Globe* and look in their morgue files and also interview people who knew Durkin in order to find out if there was "a blonde in his past," as one of my employers put it. There wasn't. Nor was there anything else of interest to the RNC.

So this was my first taste of big-time politics, and it took place one week after my memorable-only-in-retrospect first encounter with Cong. John Jenrette on the Capitol steps.

By the time John and I met again, I thought I knew everything there was to know about the somewhat tarnished inner workings of politics. I had become rather cynical—politically, at least. Nobody could pull anything over on me. History, of course, proved me wrong—in very short order.

I was working seven days a week, often until late at night. One morning, I was driving to work, bleary-eyed, as usual, and I nearly ran over John Jenrette. He stepped back, recognized me, and waved. He looked very handsome that day in a dark suit with a shirt that was the same blue color as his eyes. He asked me if I wanted to get something to eat; we lingered over lunch at the House Restaurant. That night, John took me to an Embassy party. It was my first gala in Washington, a sumptuously catered affair in the extravagantly decorated Rumanian embassy. I sensed that everybody here was somebody, although I only recognized a few senators and congressmen. The women flocking around John reminded me of the wasps that used to nest on our back porch in Texas—buzzing and hovering and every once in a while zooming in with a verbal sting, some witticism that would win the congressman's attention, make them queen for the moment of the buzzers and hoverers. I found the whole scenario thrilling. My date was a star. I was proud that a man that so many women wanted, wanted me. But after the party I dropped him off— we had driven around all day in my blue Cutlass—in front of his townhouse, and I went home where I spent the night thinking, *Well, now I've proved to that congressman-playboy that there does exist at least one woman in Washington who's not desperate to fall into bed with him.* But it was a hollow victory. My reward was a lonely night.

John, as it turned out, wasn't lonely. He told me later that after I dropped him off, he had called the Rotunda Restaurant, which is no longer in existence. The Rotunda, which was on the site of the Capitol Hill Club for the Democrats, was not just a restaurant. The man who ran the place provided call girls —and, often enough, guys—for members of Congress. The night of our first date, as John would tell me, he moonlighted with one of the Rotunda's ontap women.

Within days after the party at the Rumanian embassy, John and I were inseparable. And my RNC boss, Dick Thaxton, was incensed. As *People* magazine reported in a December 1, 1975, feature entitled "It's Romance in Washington—a Sort of Romeo and Juliet Story Amid Big-Time Politics:"

> Carpenter began making the Washington scene with Jenrette, 39, a divorcé who has led a stormy political career punctuated by lawsuits (including a rather messy divorce). He appeared politically vulnerable to the GOP, and although Rita didn't know it at the time, (RNC) researchers were trying to get something on Jenrette. What they got was Rita Carpenter. A GOP snoop staked out Jenrette's house. Sam Spade he wasn't. One morning Rita reports, "as we came out, he couldn't get his car started. He must have been playing his radio all night. We almost volunteered to help him."

I was in what is known as a compromising position. As *People* put it, "The Montagues and the Capulets were not in politics, but they would have understood the problem." The RNC's Dick Thaxton encouraged me to stop playing Juliet to John's Romeo. In short, he offered me a choice: John or my job. His reasoning was impeccable. "What would Strom Thurmond think?" he sputtered. "What would Jesse Helms think of us? If they knew our opposition research director was seeing a man who is not only a member of the opposition party but one that we have a file on this thick!" (He held up his fingers to indicate quite a sizable dossier.)

"Listen," I said, "he's not a Communist, for heaven's sake. He's only a Democrat. And I can date whomever I want to. You don't tell me who to date. or who to see. I just feel appalled."

"Well," Dick said, "I really want you to think about this because this guy has a reputation. He's— you know, I feel an obligation because I brought you up here, and now all of a sudden you're seeing this— Take the day off and decide what you're going to do, but I want you to decide to quit seeing him."

The next day, I wrote Dick a letter, as *People* tells it, and told him that I quit because nobody had the right to tell me how to live my life.

My resignation was announced in a small item in the "Chatter" column of *People* magazine. My parents saw it and called me, lamenting that they were always the last to know what was happening in my life. They thought I had made a mistake. I knew that my plans to work my way up in the Republican party had blown up in my face; not that I wanted to work for the Grand Old Party under the circumstances. In fact, I considered suing the RNC for sex discrimination and violation of the right of free association. But my lawyer talked me out of it.

After the *People* magazine item appeared in October 1975, Geraldo Rivera and *Time* magazine, among others, became interested in my love life. John's staffers were hysterical, of course, over the publicity; his constituents back in the Sixth Congressional District of South Carolina were not going to take kindly to this type of publicity. The next election was exactly one year away. And in North Myrtle Beach, South Carolina, it takes a lot longer than a year for people to forget their representative in D.C. being embarrassed on a national scale.

It is difficult to say who was more hysterical, John's worried staffers or the mortified members of the RNC. But because of all the furor—not to men-

tion fury—swirling around me, Geraldo Rivera and I
had to meet in secret. He interviewed me in La-
fayette Park one blustery afternoon and then did a
ten-minute segment on "Good Morning, America."

Meanwhile, Romeo and Juliet were not exactly the
hottest item in town; we only looked that way. For
one thing, I was now collecting unemployment,
which made the reality of my day-to-day existence
decidedly less glamorous than the media let on. John
asked me to move in to what *People* described as
"Jenrette's spiffy pad." He then took off on a business trip to Paris, at which point two of his staffers
arrived and told me, "You can't stay here. *Time*
magazine and *People* and Geraldo Rivera and everyone is trying to find you."

In the interests of pleasing John's constituents, I
moved back to my own place—but not for long.

John proposed to me during the 1976 Democratic
Convention. We were both high on New York at the
time—I had never been there before. It was an electric place, so unlike Washington. The people were
alive and uninhibited, not controlled and cautious
like the Washington crowds.

The convention consisted of party after party. I
remember them as one endless bash. All the hotel
suites, set up with liquor and snacks for the lobbyists and legislators, blur in my memory into one
hotel suite. Two events emerge, distinct, when I try
to recall that hectic, exhilarating, but exhausting
week. I met Ardeshir Zahedi, the former Iranian
ambassador to Washington and a romantic figure in
D.C. in those days, known for his lavish parties and
dating gorgerous women. It was a particularly trying evening. I felt anything but glamorous. Zahedi
pulled me out of the doldrums behind my forced

smile. He said, "I can see the moon and the stars in your eyes." For a while after that, he sent me gifts—caviar, Dom Perignon, French candies.

The second memorable moment was one I wish I could forget—and maybe one I should have taken more seriously. After we had pushed our way into the mob scene that was *Rolling Stone* magazine's party in honor of the convention, John disappeared. I found him on the roof of the building, making out with a woman who must have weighed 200 pounds. Later, he would embellish this incident, when retelling it, by claiming that the woman he was with on that roof was Shirley MacLaine. Well, she wasn't. She was a woman at whom not many men would look twice, yet there was John, in his cups and in her ample arms.

I was livid. John said he was just drunk. After all, look who he was with!

I believed John. I always believed he was faithful to me, or at least that he tried his best to be faithful, and I defended him and our relationship—because many people didn't approve of it. John's staffers discouraged him from seeing me by their attitude, if nothing else.

My friends were more direct. On one occasion, I was at a party on a yacht in the Potomac, and I was talking with Brad O'Leary, a fund raiser who had been my boss at the Republican party in Texas and who remained my friend despite the scandal when I resigned from the RNC. I was drinking a Bloody Mary, without liquor, because I seldom drink anything harder than wine. And Brad, who was very dapper, as usual—he always wears designer suits and Gucci shoes—said to me, "R.C.!" He always called me R.C. "You've really done it this time," he said. "This shmuck you're dating . . ."

"Listen," I said, "don't talk about John that way. He's a wonderful person. You don't know him."

"I do. We all know him."

At which point, I poured my Virgin Mary over his head.

So it was easy for me to overlook John's indiscretion at the *Rolling Stone* party. I loved him. It was as simple as that.

The official nomination of Jimmy Carter took place the night after the *Rolling Stone* party. That evening, as we dressed to go to Madison Square Garden, John grabbed me and held me tightly in his arms. He asked me to marry him. I couldn't resist a small joke. I asked him, "Don't you think you oughta check it out with Marvin Chernoff and your other political advisers?"

"You're right," John said. "We'll ask Marvin and Rob about it tonight at dinner."

I was flabbergasted. After the nomination, John did, indeed, consult with Marvin Chernoff and one of his political advisers. Robert Floyd. We were having dinner at *Uncle Tai's.* And over the Peking duck and Buddah's Delight, John said, "Well, guys, is it okay if I get married to Rita?"

Marvin said, "If you're planning to get married before the election, I'd say only do it if you can get Jimmy Carter to come."

Two
Washington from Five to Nine

I learned on my wedding night that a congress-man's wife cannot always count on her husband to be there when she needs him. I learned soon there-after that a congressman's wife can, however, count on her husband's demanding that she always be there when he needs her. And that being married to a congressman was a twenty-four-hour job at best.

John and I were married on September 10, 1976, in the office of the justice of the peace in Alexandria, Virginia. It was a simple ceremony. I wore a plain skirt and blouse. There were no flowers. We didn't even have a ring; we used the Marquis diamond my first husband Rick gave me. John's beeper went off before we had a chance to say "I do," summoning him back to the Capitol to vote. Jimmy Carter wasn't there.

Five hours after the ceremony, John was on a plane to South Carolina's Sixth District to campaign. The election was only two months away. He didn't ask me to go with him.

I spent my wedding night alone in our one-bed-room apartment. (John could no longer afford the "spiffy" pad.) John had rented furniture, including a mirror-embellished velvet couch and plastic lemon tree.

I cried a lot, strummed my guitar, turned the TV on, then off, returned to the guitar, picking, humming, until I found I was writing a song and that the lyrics were about John:

> You got on that jet plane
> I watched as you walked away,
> Leaving me again
> Like all the times before.

> Tonight you're in Carolina,
> And I'm here all alone,
> Wondering if you love me
> And when you're coming home.

> I gave myself to you ...

It was the emptiest night of my life. But John redeemed himself, in a way, the following week. We made up for the ruined wedding night on the steps of our nation's Capitol, where after all, John and I had met.

Congress was in late-night session. It was not unusual that as adjournment approached, they would be in session sometimes until four or five o'clock in the morning. I was at home alone when John called and asked me to meet him at the Capitol where he was waiting for me on the steps.

It was around ten P.M. John took my hand and led me behind one of the columns facing the Library of Congress. From where we were standing, I could see Tip O'Neill's limousine and his driver waiting for him. I knew what John had in mind.

We walked hand in hand up the steps to the House side of the Capitol. John then led me into the shadows of the large white columns that adorn both sides of the entranceway that members customarily use on their way to vote.

I looked into John's deep-blue eyes as he pulled me toward him. We embraced passionately; John unbuttoned my fur coat, and I fumbled with his zipper. I was wearing my blue silk skirt, and John slowly raised it above my thighs.

We wrapped my coat around us, and we made love standing in the shadow of the large column. I remember thinking how cold, very cold, it was but how warm it was next to John.

We giggled like school kids as members of Congress walked by: Moe Udall, Rick Nolan, Pete Stark, John Cavanaugh, Tom Downey, Bob Carr, walking in and out, voting.

Tip O'Neill walked by, and we waved. He said, "Hi, John. How are you?"

We both said hello to Tip.

This was the one romantic moment in the responsibility-choked first two months of our marriage. We had rebelled together, done something deliciously scandalous. We had a secret, and we needed that secret because our lives, otherwise, were an open book. There were precious few moments to be alone together, much less alone and relaxed enough to make love without feeling that we'd better hurry up before the phone rang or someone arrived on the doorstep.

I literally plummeted into the political spouse's frustrating, draining life-style, smack into the middle of John's campaign for reelection.

I became as familiar with the towns and pitstops and highways of Horry and Darlington counties, South Carolina, as I was with my Texas home town. We worked from five to nine most days, smiling nonstop, shaking hands, handing out leaflets and buttons, listening to diatribes from citizens angered about this or that, reassuring the worried citizens— Just keep John Jenrette in Congress and everything'll be fine. John made countless speeches. I engaged in endless conversations. A typical day's schedule, given to us by John's staff, went like this:

4:45 A.M.	Leave for Georgetown, South Carolina.
5:30 A.M.	Arrive Georgetown Steel Plant gate. Pass out literature.
7:15 A.M.	Go to Lafayette for breakfast. Shake hands.
8:15 A.M.	Leave for Conway.
9:30 A.M.	WJXY Radio, Hiway 378, Conway, South Carolina.
10:10 A.M.	Horry County Courthouse complex. Shake hands office to office.
11:30 A.M.	Leave for Aynor.
12:00 NOON	Aynor Manufacturing (lunch hour). Pass out literature. Shake hands.
12:30 P.M.	Leave for Marion.
1:15 P.M.	Leave Marion County Courthouse. Shake hands office to office.
2:30 P.M.	The *Monitor* newspaper (John Lewis), 301 N. Withlacoochee St., Marion, South Carolina.
3:00 P.M.	WATP Radio (Harry Hyman) 32411/2 North Main Street, Marion, South Carolina.
3:30 P.M.	Heritage plant gate.
4:15 P.M.	Leave for Conway.
5:00 P.M.	*Horry Independent* newspaper (Steve Robertson), 3rd Avenue, Conway, South Carolina.
5:45 P.M.	Leave for Myrtle Beach.

And the dinners, cocktails, benefit picnics, speech-making, and staff strategy meetings often lasted long into the night with or without me). And the drinking—occasionally, John got so plastered that I couldn't imagine how he'd be up smiling and shaking hands the next day. Yet he always was. And the drinking, after all, was part of the politician's way of life, part of socializing with the voters and backers, being one of the boys. It also helped John to unwind.

The drinking was a small flaw that I figured I had to put up with. In any case, the exhilaration of campaigning with this man, who had done so much for his district—and it was written all over the faces of the people who supported him—was so enormous that his occasional drunkenness didn't bother me. If anything, it made him seem more virile, more of that sort of man who, by his very obvious preeminence in that exclusive world of maleness, is often beyond the reach, physically and otherwise, of his wife and is therefore all the more desirable.

I was intensely proud of him. In his unsuccessful 1972 bid for Congress, he had defeated, in the Democratic primary, John L. McMillan, who had been in office for thirty-three years and who was a segregationist. My husband, I quickly gathered, had a Kennedylike aura for the blacks, who comprised 42 percent of the population of his district. When I went into homes in the poorer areas of Horry County, I saw John Jenrette's picture right up there next to photographs of Robert and John Kennedy. And he had earned their support and affection, starting affirmative-action programs and putting blacks in positions of authority on his staff. It was the first time that the black people of Horry County had had a real voice in Washington. John worked hard for improvements in social security policies and voted to censor Rhodesia for its segregationist policies. He was a real firebrand for a Southern politician.

He won the election. But any exhilaration I felt, any pride in my part in his victory, was wiped out in the raucous course of the celebations. John, boisterous, flushed, primed by alcohol, was mobbed by well-wishers, many of them equally tipsy. Everyone was pulling on him. There were all these voices, loud voices, women grabbing at him—men, too—and the smell of alcohol everywhere. It was overpowering. And bright lights. And every once in a while a voice louder than the rest: "Boy, I just love you, John Jenrette, y'all come over to our house just any time, y'hear?"

I felt as if I were watching a grade B movie and that somehow I had a peripheral role in it. In another sense, however, it was as if I weren't really there. I felt nothing. There was no personal gratification; no one was patting me on the back; no one was telling me, "Good job; you worked hard." Not even John. He never said, "Rita, come stand by me." I felt so betrayed. I felt as if he were ashamed of me. I thought, *Well, maybe I didn't do a good job.* I had worked from four A.M. till two A.M. for so many days over the last two months—but maybe I hadn't been effective.

And although I knew that my life shouldn't be contingent on my husband's, that it shouldn't revolve around him, that I should have my own career and goals—and I wanted to succeed on my own as something—I still ended up, when that long night was over, feeling that I had failed.

So I told myself that next time I would campaign harder. I'd do better.

Later, alone in our hotel room, I tried to tell John how I felt. We had a good marriage. We could talk, I thought. But he was reeling from the liquor and the victory, and he told me that I was too possessive. He said I had to accept the fact that he was a public figure and that women were going to kiss him and that people were going to hang on to him. And he couldn't, for heaven's sake, with all these people rushing him, look out for me.

We were up and running at five the next morning after two hours' sleep. The election was over. The post election thank-you's had begun. I had thought that that morning we'd lie around in bed, make love, have breakfast brought to our room, and relax and enjoy the victory. But no. By six A.M., we were shaking hands in front of a Dixie cup factory—what is known in political parlance as "doing a plant gate." I felt like a robot standing there, shaking hands, saying, "Thank you for voting for my husband." Those people didn't want to shake my hand any more than I wanted to be there. And what if some of the people I thanked hadn't even voted for John? They'd be snickering behind our backs. I felt like a fool. And still John didn't thank me for my work.

Then after several days of thank-yous, we were back on the Hill in Washington, back to a grind of another sort.

We had begun our life together with very little income. Much of John's $60,000 a year salary went to his ex-wife. I took a job working for Sen. Hubert Humphrey at the Office of Technology Assessment (OTA), compiling a study on the transfer of food to developing nations. The World Food Hunger Commission relies on the information in this study to this day. And the household grew: John's eleven-year-old son, Hal, came to live with us for a while. He slept on the velvet couch in the living room.

I was enjoying my research with the OTA—the

project was something I'm proud to have worked on. But my work, which was contributing considerably to maintaining our always-behind-the-eight-ball way of life, was being undermined by the social obligations that were built into John's position. The Washington party-go-round! It picked me up like a tornado and showed me a glittering new world. I felt like Dorothy in Oz, at first. And like Dorothy in Oz, I would eventually want to go home. But for now I was awed and fascinated. We'd go to dinner, and I'd be sitting across from people who were names in headlines, staring into faces I knew from *Time* and *Newsweek* and *People*, from movies and television.

My years as John Jenrette's wife were nothing if not star studded. One day it was a luncheon for Bette Davis in one of the private rooms in the Capitol. She was crusty, outspoken, mischievous. Her eyes sparkled with the sheer joy of living. She was everything I'd someday like to be. Another day it was a luncheon at the Smithsonian for members of the "All in the Family" family. Sally Struthers, Rob Reiner, Jean Stapleton, and producer Norman Lear. Unfortunately, Archie himself, Carroll O'Connor, was unable to be there because he was ill—even more unfortunate because the purpose of the function was the donation of Archie's chair to the Smithsonian. There is now a special place in the museum for the chair, which is surrounded by a set from the show. At lunch, John sat next to Jean Stapleton, whom he liked a great deal.

But as memorable as getting to chat with the stars of everyone's favorite sit-com at the reception that evening was Eunice Shriver's reception of me. I had helped Eunice with a fund raiser she had given in 1976 when Sarge was trying to do away with the debts he had acquired during his vice presidential race with George McGovern. And Eunice and I had developed a good rapport. But that night, when Eunice, who was dressed modestly, as usual—she is always impeccably ladylike—saw me coming in my low-cut black dress, she pulled on Sarge's arm, and they walked away.

It was not the first time, nor would it be the last, that I was snubbed in Washington. I shrugged the incident off, but it still hurt.

Another memorable occasion was the Moroccan embassy reception following a Liza Minelli concert at Kennedy Center. I talked for quite a while with the most interesting men there—Andy Warhol—who was so intent on observing the Washington crowd, undoubtedly a far cry from the New York jet setters he's used to, that I was sure he would go home and figure out some way to put protocol on canvas!

I met Elizabeth Taylor several times, but the first was when she was being "roasted" at the Saints and Sinners Luncheon. This charity affair is put on every so often; the draw is, of course, the celebrity they're roasting. Naturally, all Washington showed up for Elizabeth Taylor. She was in a wheelchair, obviously in great pain, although nobody seemed to know why. She was carried on to the stage, wheelchair and all. I was surprised at how short she is and how petite—despite the catty comments about her legendary weight problem from some of the socialites in attendance. "Isn't she fat?" was about the kindest comment. And I looked at Elizabeth Taylor's critics, the local crème de la crème, with their sunken cheeks and wrinkles—they're all bone thin, fashion-harpie thin—and chuckled to myself. Because all the men in the room—their husbands included—were ogling Elizabeth Taylor. And all I could think of was how jealous these women were because Elizabeth Taylor really is exquisite and they'd just been waiting for her to put on five pounds so they could feel superior to her. But not one woman in that room could touch her. She has the most perfectly symmetrical face, with those eyes that really are more violet than blue and that glorious black hair. But beyond that, she has a sense of humor, and when I chatted with her, her intelligence and inner strength were apparent.

I never met, and never would meet, a woman with the qualities I sensed in Elizabeth Taylor until I attended a luncheon for Mrs. Anwar Sadat. Both Elizabeth Taylor and Mrs. Sadat radiate incredible strength of character. I admire them more than words can say—they've been through it all, and they're survivors.

I wore a gypsy outfit to the luncheon for Mrs. Sadat—a silk antique skirt with a little vest and a silk blouse. The other congressional wives were dressed in prim and proper suits. They gave me the once over, of course. Mrs. Sadat was more gracious; unlike our luncheon companions, she did not judge people according to whether their taste in clothes conformed to hers. We talked for quite a while about women's rights, about some of the problems that she was involved with at that time in Egypt, about her sympathy for Farah Diba—this was after the fall of the shah of Iran—suddenly homeless, exiled, with a sick husband. But that topic of conversation ended abruptly when someone, presumably a reporter, walked up to us.

Another wife of a head of state, Margaret Trudeau, impressed me in quite a different way. We met once at the Capitol and again at a function at the White House. She was wearing a very expensive suit and a huge fur hat—I'll never forget that hat; it overwhelmed her. I spoke to her in the receiving line; she seemed not to really see me. But her response to everyone else was similar—preoccupied or aloof, detached, even disoriented. Looking back, I realize that this function was probably the last public function that she attended before leaving her husband Pierre.

John and I visited the White House frequently, so I had more than a nodding acquaintance with Rosalyn Carter. She was always reserved, always in complete control, always the perfect political wife. She never said anything that could be misjudged. I got the feeling that all her moves were rather calculated and deliberate. I never felt any warmth from her.

I'll never forget the evening when John and I attended a Willie Nelson concert at the White House. During the Carters' reign at the White House, one never quite knew what to wear. Initially, Jimmy Carter refused to wear a black tie. Therefore, everyone felt—but nobody was ever sure—that it would be okay to show up at the White House dressed casually. Then, when Carter received criticism for never wearing a tuxedo, he apparently decided that the American people really didn't want to see their president attired in blue jeans and carrying his own suitcase. So he started wearing tuxedos now and then. But one never knew. So there was always the risk that if you went casual to the White House, because Carter had been casual the time before, he might show up formal.

I chose a long dress for the Willie Nelson concert. John dressed up, too. We arrived and discovered that the concert—which I looked forward to because I'd been a great Willie Nelson fan even if I wasn't from Texas—was on the lawn of the White House. John and I felt somewhat overdressed. We were seated at a table with three men who had just crossed the Atlantic in a hot-air baloon. We chatted about their adventure, how many close calls they had had, and they were really fascinating. Then Rosalyn sat down with us.

This event took place when the Egypt-Israel agreements were underway, with Sadat, Begin, and Carter conferring at Camp David. And Rosalyn had flown in to make an appearance. The three balloonists tried to talk with her, and John and I tried to talk with her. She was gracious but just barely so. More or less like a block of ice. At first, I thought she was reacting adversely to being dressed for grand opera when the performer was a country singer. Then, observing her icy demeanor—she had a smile pasted on her face like a little doll—I knew that it couldn't just be my dress that was bothering her.

It was well known that Rosalyn had a big hand in the Carter administration. She sat in on cabinet meetings—that was a first for a president's wife. It was known that she even changed some public policy. Some decisions that the president made were based on Rosalyn's impressions. Now Carter and Begin and Sadat were on the verge of a breakthrough in the Middle East crisis. So I suppose that for Rosalyn, having been in Camp David where the action was, having to go to the White House for this little party was probably quite irritating.

Another encounter I had with Rosalyn Carter—rather, a nonencounter—was just after John and I were married. I tried to enlist her support to help in the passage of the Equal Rights Amendment (ERA) in South Carolina. At that point, we only needed two more states for the ERA to pass.

John was very brave about the ERA. He sent a letter to each state legislature asking them to support it. Rosalyn had professed to support it, but when I asked her to travel to South Carolina with me to help put it over the top, I really received the runaround from one of her secretaries. I was astounded. Betty Ford would have gone in one second flat.

Although the Fords left the White House soon after I became a congressional wife, I did get to meet them, and I was impressed with their genuineness, their sincerity. Ford didn't have the polish that so many presidents before and after him have had. That was what was so delightful about him—his down-to-earthness. It's also probably why he didn't win in 1976. Americans demand in their presidents the pizzazz that televison puts over. That's how we choose to vote or not vote for someone—not on the basis of genuine concern about this country, which Ford had in abundance. So did his wife.

At a Christmas party during their years in the White House, everyone was whispering about Mrs. Ford's drinking and drug problems. Nobody had written about it at that point. They said that she was on medication for her arthritic condition.

I found her fantastically open, refreshing in every way. And I think that Ford's losing the election probably saved her life and their marriage. He had been the minority leader of the House of Representatives, after all, before becoming Nixon's vice president, then president. I guess the way she dealt with her husband's public success was through alcohol and pills, common balms for political wives. But she was able to admit to the world that she had these problems, and she was able to conquer them. I had the utmost respect and esteem for Betty Ford. And, of course, since I believe in candor myself, I certainly admire her *chutzpah* to be able to go out there and be so open.

Jody Powell was also remarkably honest, all-around nice—probably my favorite Carter-administration person. He was once supposed to come to a fund raiser for John; throughout the function, he kept calling and saying, "Well, I can't come yet . . . there's a crisis brewing . . . you'll read about it in the *Post* tomorrow, and then you'll know . . ." The next day, the *Post* described the full-blown Cuban refugee problem, and we knew that that was what Jody had been talking about.

Joan Mondale was among the more taciturn figures in the Carter administration. I found her to be prim-looking, neat, quite thin, and highly intelligent—similar in some ways to Rosalyn Carter but without the icy edge. I met Mrs. Mondale at National Airport. She was going to South Carolina with John and me to campaign for Charles Dufort "Pug" Ravenel, who was running against Strom Thurmond, senior Republican senator from South Carolina. When Mrs. Mondale walked briskly into the Piedmont VIP lounge at the airport, I quickly stood and shook her hand. I asked her if she would be kind enough to allow me to interview her. I planned to write up the interview for a magazine or a newspaper. At that time, I was toying with the idea of seeing if I could write and, perhaps, getting into journalism. I was always trying to establish some sort of career goal for myself by way of trying to establish an identity apart from my career as John's wife. At this moment, I thought writing sounded like a good idea.

Mrs. Mondale seemed quite tense. I asked her about the Camp David accords. She looked agitated. It became clear that she would discuss the arts and only the arts. Although it was obvious that this intelligent woman was capable of grasping and talking about the Camp David accords or anything else I asked her about, she skillfully steered our conversation away from controversy.

Throughout our campaign tour in South Carolina,

during the receptions, fund-raising events, and speaking engagements, I thought Mrs. Mondale was weighing each and every word she said.

I admired her for her discipline, for the grace with which she carried out the role of vice president's wife and accepted the personal restraints that went with it. I wondered if she sometimes felt, as I did, that she *was* constrained or if she longed, as I did, to suddenly cut loose in public, say what she felt regardless of whether or not it reflected well on her husband, and damn the torpedoes! But I never had the nerve to ask her.

When I look back on my Washington years, my meeting with Mrs. Sadat was one of the two truly stellar moments. The other highlight, an event I remember with great satisfaction, was during the first month of my marriage. One of the items on my campaign schedule—John and I did not always operate in tandem—was visiting a Meals on Wheels Program for elderly people. I went early one morning with one of John's staffers to the address we were given, in a rural community. When we entered the building, it soon became obvious that the word "meals" was a gross exaggeration. The senior citizens, most of them in their eighties or nineties, most of them black, were being fed a watery sort of soup made out of fat. I was appalled.

John's staffer accompanied me to a nearby grocery store. We bought about a hundred dollars worth of bread and cheese and meat and took the food back to the senior citizens. Seeing their faces when they looked at all that food was probably the high point of my entire congressional experience. There were several other times when my position as a congressman's wife enabled me to help people I otherwise couldn't have helped. I arranged, for instance, for a South Carolinian whose daughter had a birth defect to meet with the top plastic surgeon at Johns Hopkins.

As John's wife, I initiated a number of programs in South Carolina. The first was the Sunflower Program. Through my work with the OTA on the transfer of food to developing nations, I started a project that made sunflowers an alternate crop to tobacco in South Carolina. And, with Dick Gregory and Muhammad Ali, I worked to initiate a nutrition program in the Sixth District. Dick Gregory and I went down to the district and held nutrition seminars for school superintendents and nutritionists. I donated a number of works of art to the Florence Museum, and through the Department of Health, Education and Welfare I laid the groundwork for a more comprehensive state museum and arts program. And much of my time in the district was spent in giving lectures, speeches, or talks; on occasion, too, I would sing, at benefits especially for the South Carolina Cancer Society in which I was active. Although I had not yet sung professionally, I had sung and written songs all my life.

But, for the most part, my role as Mrs. Congressman Jenrette was that of John's appendage. The parties, which had been such a thrill at first, soon became as routine as going out and shopping for groceries and about as glamorous as scrubbing your bathroom floor. There were five receptions a night, nearly every night of the week. Some people might find it hard to believe that one can actually tire of champagne and caviar, but I did, quickly.

Washington parties, unlike Hollywood parties and New York parties, have a sameness that is almost laughable. I know that in other centers of power, hosts and hostesses will choose unusual locations for their bash—a roller disco, say, or a bohemian loft or

a strip of beach or even a city street! In Washington,—in political circles, at least—parties take place
either in hotel ballrooms, in embassies, or in penthouse suites at the Watergate. There are, basically,
several categories of parties that congressmen fre-
quent. There are the receptions given by lobbyists.
Let's say Rockwell International has given you the
congressman, the maximum—a $5,000 campaign
contribution. You, the congressman, then have to
show up when Rockwell gives a Washington reception because Rockwell brings in big wheels from
L.A. and New York to attend their reception, and
it is important, for the lobbyist who handed you
that campaign contribution, that you, the congressman, be there—with your wife. So that is one kind
of reception.

Then there are the parties given by the telephone
company, and the electric co-op, and other powerful
forces in your home district.

Then various manufacturers and businesses hold
their once-a-year shindig in Washington, and their
congressman has to show up. So does his wife. It
doesn't matter that you have five other receptions,
to go to at the same time. Somehow you have to
attend them all.

John and I developed a game that we would play
at receptions. I would say, "Y'know, we've gotta go
now." And John would say, "Oh, I don't want to
leave right now." And I'd reply, "Well, you know we
really have to be at..." And I'd name whatever
place was next on the agenda. And then we'd go to
the next party.

John and I had been married a very short time
when we attended a reception at the Hyatt Regency.
It was a group from John's district. They asked us
upstairs to the Hospitality Room where VIP's were
served drinks. John never turned down an invitation

to the Hospitality Room. And I started playing our little game. "John," I said, "we've gotta go now." And John said, "Well, all right . . ." And while I was waiting for him to make the first move toward the door, a man who was sitting on the couch, drunk, and had obviously overhead me nagging John to leave spoke to me: "D'you think you're the most important thing to him?" he asked.

"Listen," I said, "I would never presume to ask your wife there if you're the most important thing to her, or vice-versa. How can you be so presumptuous as to ask me that. Of course, I'm the most important thing to him!"

I believed that with all my heart. John was attentive. He supported us. He was generous and romantic, leaving me little love notes on the refrigerator and elsewhere around the house. He remembered to bring home six-packs of my favorite Diet Dr. Pepper.

It was worth it that my responsibilities as his wife were cutting into my own responsibilities, working for the OTA. I found, more and more, that I couldn't continue with my work in the area of transferring of food-processing technology to developing nations. In my role as a congressional spouse, John would want me to leave sometimes on a Thursday when Congress adjourned and head off to the district. I not only had to attend recentions with John at night; there were also functions during the day at which I had to represent him. Soon I became a consultant to the OTA, working part time. Finally, I couldn't justify putting such minimal effort into what I thought was a valuable project. So I left OTA and completely immersed myself in the role of John's wife.

But this, too, was valuable, I told myself. Our relationship was solid as a rock. John was totally devoted to me despite intimations to the contrary that seemed to crop up—at the 1976 Christmas party in Georgetown, South Carolina, for instance, when a woman started screaming at John, "You goddamn bastard!" And I was standing there in a long dress, trying to act like a congressman's wife.

"What do you have going with that woman?" I asked John.

"Oh, look, before we were married, if I were in Georgetown, I'd call her and— But we weren't married then, Rita. Now I'd never look at her twice."

I believed him.

John and I went to North Myrtle Beach, South Carolina, about a month after our first wedding anniversary not only for the usual campaigning—even when there's no election, politicians campaign constantly—but to relax together, however briefly. I was feeling proud of myself, a person in my own right, for the first time in months. The day before we went to Myrtle Beach, I had been in New York, modeling for some print ads for Clairol's Clairesse campaign. It was quite an experience. Clairol sent me to Leslie Blanchard, an internationally known hair colorist, to have my hair sun streaked—I had shoulder-length straight hair then—and curled. It looked different but beautiful. Eventually, I toured the country for Clairol. It was a unique experience campaigning for Clairesse instead of for John.

John had come to New York with me. He wanted to see what the advertising world was like. (Actually, it reminded me a lot of politics. Everything revolved around selling the product. As Jim Goff, one of John's campaign advisers, once told me, "I can get anybody elected as long as he keeps his mouth shut and his wife's mouth shut and stays out of the way. With the right money and the right TV spots, I can get anybody in this country elected.")

So we had flown from New York straight to Myrtle Beach. There were a lot of parties that night. We finally wound up, very late, at the home of a friend where we were spending the night in the guest house. Two women were visiting at the time, and shortly after we arrived, it became obvious to me that one of them was coming on to John. I thought, *Well, who cares? She's older than my own mother.* She was white-haired, with a lot of lines on her face. She was also drunk. John proceeded to get drunk, too. When we finally retired to the guest house, I was feeling romantic. We had just celebrated our first anniversary, after all. But John ignored me.

I tried to remain objective. He was drunk; it wasn't that he didn't love me anymore. I had just read Dr. Wayne Dyer's book *How to Pull Your Own Strings,* which was full of sound advice on being your own person. And that was the way I was feeling, buoyed by my experience with Clairol. I figured I would go with the flow. I went to sleep.

At around four A.M., I woke up. John wasn't in the bed. *Oh, no,* I thought. *He's passed out in the main house. I'd better go and get him.* I put on my jeans. This was the first day of my new philosophy, the new me as created by Dr. Wayne Dyer's words. So I went over to the main house, and there was one of the elderly women sitting half asleep in front of the videotape machine. The picture was over; the screen was snowy but I could still see what the tape was. *Deep Throat.* I asked the woman where John was. And where was her friend?

"Well, I think they went for a walk on the beach."

I was beginning to get angry. We had been married for a whole year, and John had never gone to the beach with me. He'd never taken time to walk with me on the beach at midnight. Now he was out at four in the morning with some old bag, walking on the beach.

I jumped in a car—I don't know whose; the key was in the ignition—and drove down to the beach. It never occurred to me that it might be dangerous walking around the beach alone at four A.M. I just had to witness this event for myself: John walking along with this woman on the beach. The idea that he might be doing anything sexual with this woman was unimaginable.

They were nowhere to be found.

I returned to the house and went upstairs. Our host and hostess were asleep. I looked in some of the other rooms. Then I remembered this door that looked as if it led to the outside but didn't. I approached the door and heard voices. I flipped the light switch on, pulling the curtain on the door and looking through the little window.

There was John, completely nude. The woman was also nude.

I went berserk. My new philosophy—that I had to stop being possessive and paranoid and give John space—went out the window. Literally. I kicked in one of the windowpanes and punched out another one. My arm and leg were bleeding. When John finally opened the door, which was chained, I hit him. He said, "You caught me," or something, and I hit him.

I jumped in the car and drove around the streets of Myrtle Beach, on to the highway, going the wrong way, screaming at the top of my lungs. I heard myself screaming, but it sounded like someone else.

I ended up at John's sister's house. She patched up my cuts and gashes. The next day, I left for Washington.

John's staff sprang into action. They put John on a plane for Washington. He didn't even bring his clothes with him. That night, he showed up on our doorstep, begging my forgiveness. "Please forgive me. I've never done anything like this in my life. You're the most important thing in the world to me."

Once again, I believed him. Don't you believe the one you love? Don't you want to?

And yet I began to realize, slowly and painfully, that although living as John's wife could be romantic, excitive, filled with celebrities and glamor, I would never be anything more than John's wife. I was no longer Rita. I was simply the woman on John's right arm. And, as I was beginning to realize also, not the only woman there. Sure I was the woman who was there when the cameras were, when John was on stage, but who knew about what other women were there when I wasn't? I was aware that the other Congressmen and Senators were having sex with people other than their wives; I just couldn't believe John was. Well, maybe, when he was drunk. But just the few times I caught him. I really believed that I caught him every time.

I should have guessed that if he hadn't gotten away with it sometimes, he wouldn't do it ever, for it was the times he got away with it that made him do it again.

Three

Washington
AC to DC

My friend Jane sat across from me at Duddington's, confessing her sins. I hadn't seen her for a while. She had come to Washington and gotten a good job with a Southern congressman. We were fairly close, but after a while, she stopped calling. I was a little hurt. I thought that perhaps because I was now a congressman's wife, she was intimidated.

I finally called her. We met for a glass of wine one evening at Duddington's, a popular restaurant on the Hill where Capitol staffers hang out. The place was crowded and noisy. Jane kept her head lowered so no one could see her tears as she talked. And her voice was low. I strained to hear her. When I got the gist of what she was saying, I understood why she did not want to risk being overheard.

She hadn't called me, she said, because she didn't know what to say to me. She thought I had heard about what she had been involved in.

"What, for heaven's sake?" I asked her.

She told me that a top aide of the congressman she worked for had been forcing her to go to parties. At the first party, people were taking off their clothes at the door. She was forced to participate in sexual acts. If she didn't cooperate, she was told, she would lose her job. The idea of losing her job terrified her since she had moved thousands of miles to Washington to start a career and had no money of her own.

The party scene wasn't all Jane told me about. She was also forced to go out with constituents when they came into town—usually much older, fat, sloppy men.

They would go to parties where clothing and shoes were stacked haphazardly across the room; people were in various states of intimacy, some two, three, or four to a group. Jane thought they reminded her of trapeze artists. But she knew she had to go along with whatever anyone asked her to do.

I was incredulous. But when I asked John about it, he said that before we were married, he'd been to a few orgies himself. I couldn't believe it. And then, when I appeared on Carol Randolph's "Morning Break" show in Washington, a viewer called in and said that all the above was true, that this (unidentified) viewer owned a massage parlor on 14th Street and that her client's list read like a *Who's Who* of American politics. The prominent senators and congressmen on this list, she said, could replace the *Green Book* (Washington's list of elite).

Not long after this meeting with Jane at Duddington's, I heard that she had left this particular congressional office. She's now involved in another Washington job. I was happy to hear this. She had gotten out by the skin of her teeth. Other women have not been so lucky.

Although it was some time before I became thoroughly disillusioned with my husband, my disenchantment with Washington set in within a year after my marriage. I guess, like everyone else, there are certain groups of people I idealize, if not idolize.

Even after Watergate, I had a rosy view of politicians, not unlike the image one has of one's family doctor. Certain people are supposed to be more virtuous than the rest of the population. Some congressmen and senators undoubtedly are. Too many, unfortunately, aren't.

I guess I had known from the first time I set foot in Washington that it was, for one thing, a bastion of male chauvinism. I was struck by the hypocrisy of legislators who, after all, are making rules for the rest of the country on equal rights for women (not to mention other minorities) yet in their own world discriminate beyond belief. They don't seem to have to adhere to the very laws they enact. If a female employee of a congressman has a grievance against her employer, there's little she can do about it. Nowadays, the situation has improved somewhat. The women's organizations have helped to an extent. Still, if you want to keep your job on the Hill, you take the discrimination. You keep your mouth shut, and you work. For some women, these jobs— for which they are paid less than men in equivalent positions—are worth the sacrifice of their equal rights. And other sacrifices.

I got to know the comings and goings of certain congressmen in a way that the people who elect them seldom do. Their wives talked with me; their girl friends talked with me. I began compiling my own congressional record.

There was a congressman who resigned from office; he received national publicity when he announced, with tears in his eyes, his resignation. It was all very moving. So was the nonpublicized side of the story, the saga of his administrative assistant. He had lived with this woman. He paid her a good salary, and from her salary she paid for their very nice apartment. Shortly after the congressman announced that he was resigning, he beat up his administrative assistant/lover with a baseball bat to such an extent that she had to be hospitalized. Everyone in Washington knew of their relationship and even about the beating, including some reporters. Yet nobody talked about the incident. It went unreported.

After the woman recovered from the beating, this congressman got her another, better job with a lobbyist. Since she values this job, she's never talked about the violent end of her affair. And a man that had interceded on her behalf and tried to protect her is now, thanks to the congressman, working in a bureaucratic agency, earning $40,000 a year. Naturally, he's not about to tell the world about the family-man congressman's darker side.

Meanwhile, the congressman went on to have an affair with another female member of his staff.

This man, incidentally, is a hero of the moral majority, and he is now contemplating running for political office again.

I really think that there is a certain type of man who is attracted to politics and that often that person is suffering from deep and severe sexual identity problems. As Myra McPherson says in her book *The Power Lovers,* most of our political leaders are ex-high school presidents who couldn't get it up. I came to believe that that is more true than not. Some of the congressmen and senators who are seen as the Don Juans of the Hill actually have severe sexual problems.

I know of a congressman who was divorcing his wife (or was she divorcing him?). He took a very beautiful young woman to one of the Caribbean islands. They went scuba diving. The more aerobically fit you are, of course, the longer you can stay under water. So the beautiful young woman and the congressman dove into the water, taking an instructor with them. The congressman had to come up rather quickly since he was not in top shape. He left his girl friend underwater with the instructor, and they repaired to a cave where they took off their gear and made wild, passionate love.

When they surfaced, the congressman said to his young lady friend and to the scuba-diving instructor, "Gee, you guys are really fit."

According to the young woman, this congressman was as unfit in bed as he was underwater. He attributed this to his breakup with his wife.

Then there's the senator who is known as quite a ladies' man. He took a friend of mine to his home after a party. He did not or could not make love to her. At the crack of dawn, he jumped out of bed, put on his shorts, and said he was going jogging. My friend waited around for him. Finally, seven hours later, around noon, she figured out that he probably wasn't coming back.

Washington is not only full of women who have been victimized by their employers' pulling them into the town's secret sexual whirlpool. There are women who come to Washington looking for a good time—political groupies. I call them "lurkers," a more descriptive term. Lurkers—once they've caught on to the system—try to snare the more powerful legislators. You have a lot more status within the Hill system if you're having an affair with a prime mover than with a lowly freshman member of the Senate or the House. In Washington, women gain status according to how powerful a man they're sleeping with. Because many of these men are married, the liaisons often occur in borrowed apartments—and less predictable places. I know of three or four senators who rent a house near the Senate office building for "nooners." Quickies also take place in certain rooms in the bowels of the Capitol, rooms that are supposed to be for meetings. Some of these political gathering places are, however, equipped with comfortable couches. Congressman and senators also have a defense program that has never come up on the floor. According to my husband, a staffer at the House of Representatives keeps a supply of condoms on hand for legislators en route to a quickie.

I discovered this when John came home with one of these congressional condoms in his pocket. He told me he had procured it as a joke. He owed another congressman money. He had filled the condom with quarters and presented it to the congressman—and then kept the condom. Of course, I accepted his story as I always did. I was unaware, at the time, that John had been using a friend's Sixth Street apartment several times a week for his own liaisons.

This was also before I was almost seduced into Washington's *underground* party-go-round, the night that a White House staffer invited John and me to his house. John had had too much to drink. I had also had a drink during our dinner at the Democratic Club. When we arrived at this man's house—he had invited us to "see my redecorating job"—the man proceeded to drug my drink. Then he put something under my nose that almost made me black out and proceeded to try to seduce me with my husband sitting right there, albeit in a drunken stuper. I could hardly see, but I managed somehow to rouse John from his stupor. We wobbled to the door and managed to get home.

The man who drugged me and tried to seduce me didn't stop there. He called me after that horrendous night and said, "Would you like to go out with me? We'll see each other alone and not tell John."

I said, "Absolutely not. I never want to see you

again. John and I are not like you." This man had a girl friend who had worked at the Department of Energy. She was reputed to be a nymphomaniac who serviced members of Congress.

Some ambitious women in Washington court politicians not merely for social status but for political mileage. Their shenanigans, in other words, are all part of a day's, or night's, work. One story that got around town rather quickly concerned a female lobbyist for a large defense contracter during the time the company was trying to get federal funding for their B-1 bomber. This lobbyist met Hamilton Jordan at a party for Pug Ravenel, Strom Thurmond's opponent in his last bid for reelection. Hamilton had just separated from his wife and was coming on to the lobbyist. He asked her to take him back to the White House.

"Oh, sure," said the dreamy-eyed lobbyist.

She and Hamilton left the reception. All the other lobbyists were furious because they wanted to be able to talk to Hamilton and push their own projects for presidential consideration. The female lobbyist, who was a bit tipsy, drove Hamilton to the White House. She then returned to the party, undoubtedly confident that her company would get its federal funding.

But the following week, Hamilton worked overtime to defeat the B-1 bomber. And he and president Carter succeeded in defeating it.

Another female lobbyist, is said—by a reliable member of the press—to have videotapes of herself and friends *in flagrante delicto* with various Republican congressmen and senators. This woman's husband, also a lobbyist, apparently encouraged her to sleep with these men not merely to get legislation favoring issues that concerned them but to "get" the politicians. It is said, also, that this woman claims to have had an abortion that was paid for in part by a Republican senator who voted for the Hyde Amendment, which limited federal funding for abortions.

What errant congressmen and senators cannot get for free, they pay for. John was not the only legislator who had a call girl whom he called upon to "date" visiting constituents and lobbyists. During the period right before John and I were married, Suzy Thompson Park, as the reigning queen of the political parties, set up congressmen and senators with girl friends. She was Carl Albert's top aide herself, of course. She wielded a lot of power. One evening, John took me to a party she had invited him to at a Chinese restaurant in Alexandria, Virginia. Also attending the dinner were a number of high-class call girls and quite a few members of Congress—without their wives. The men were obviously being serviced by these women. It was a scene I won't quickly forget, the tall, glamorous girls standing there like mannequins with the politicians scurrying around, choosing among them.

It would seem that Washington is a very sexy town. But there isn't really that much real sex in the underground political party-go-round. It's a façade of sex. Most of the time, the Hill's Don Juans, the men who are considered the Warren Beatties of the political world, are sexually insecure. If you're secure about your sexuality, you don't have to go around trying to prove to everyone that you have a penis. It seems that some of our country's lawmakers are titillated only in an orgy situation.

A very large number of legislators are gay. The Longworth "Tea Room" is a bathroom facility that is known, and has been known for years, on the Hill as the place where congressmen, senators, or staffers go if they want to have a homosexual liaison. It had been rumored for years that incidents were taking place there. But the first arrest that was ever made in the tea room was when Cong. Jon Clifton Hinson, of Mississippi, was caught there in February 1981 with a twenty-eight-year-old staffer from the Library of Congress.

This was not the first time that Congressman Hinson had been caught in a homosexual act. There had been two previous incidents. There was a fire in a local gay film club a few years ago in which a staffer from a South Carolina congressman's office was killed. Several other Hill people were present, among them Congressman Hinson. He was caught again at another of Washington's gay hangouts, the Iwo Jima Memorial, and was arrested, then released. He then narrowly won reelection after claiming he had been born again and had seen the light. Then came his arrest at the Longworth tea room.

Congressman Bob Bauman, of Maryland, like Hinson, was a favorite of the moral majority. No one could have been farther to the right than Bauman except Attila the Hun. He was against every single liberal reform, against abortion, and vehemently antigay. He was caught molesting an underaged boy. Agents had been watching him for quite a while. He frequented gay establishments around Washington, driving his car with congressional plates.

Being gay, of course, is no more a crime than being heterosexual. The nature of these legislators' sex lives is not the issue here. It's the way they went about conducting their liaisons in public. And it's their hypocrisy. Bob Bauman would stride on to the floor of the House and pound the desk and carry on an antigay tirade in the manner of Anita Bryant. Then he'd go out at night carousing in gay bars. I found this hypocrisy to be appalling.

Bauman and Hinson are far from being the only homosexual legislators; there are two senators from the very same state who are gay. Both of them are vehemently antihomosexual in public. Both of them support the moral majority. Both of them carry on a great façade of heterosexuality with some of Washington's sexiest women. The women may be well aware of the truth about these men, but they would never reveal it. They want to be written up in the gossip columns of the *Washington Star* and the *Washington Post*. So they go along with the act.

Hinson's track record in particular indicates something disturbing about congressmen as a whole. Having been caught two times in homosexual activities in public and after winning reelection, anyway, he *still* risked going to a bathroom facility on Capitol Hill to engage in a homosexual act. What happens is that when a congressman or senator wins reelection, he becomes even more enveloped in the aura of Washington and his own self-importance. He seems to feel omnipotent, as if he is beyond the norms of right and wrong, that he can make his own rules and function as he wants to function.

Amazingly, the wives of Congressmen Hinson and Bauman still stand by their husbands. My heart goes out to them, and perhaps their loyalty should not come as such a surprise to me because, as it turned out, I stuck by my husband, too, after his behavior had caused me agony in private and embarrassment in public. And if some people question why I stayed with John for such a long time, I'd tell them to ask Mrs. Hinson and Mrs. Bauman the same question.

In fact, my loyalty to John was such that even after I had become all too aware that he was not the most high-principled of men, I was shocked by the revelations of another congressional wife. She was around my age. When I first met her, she was newly married and deliriously happy. A few years later, she had become a totally different person. The bitterness in her voice and the jaded look in her eyes as she described the decline of her marriage told me that the energetic young wife I had once known had become a disillusioned, beaten-down woman. She said that she had learned to function totally as a single parent. She didn't need her husband. She no longer campaigned for him. In fact, "the less he comes home the better."

In one sense, this attitude could be interpreted as a declaration of independence, the game plan of a newly liberated woman. But this woman was not "liberated"; she was lonely. She hadn't asked to be so independent, after all. She was acting—and speaking—out of bitterness rather than self-esteem.

Another congressional spouse that I was close to left her husband after he started bringing call girls to their home. She had put up with his cocaine addiction. She had even gone with him to massage parlors on 14th St. in a misbegotton effort to save their marriage. When she told me what she had been through, I was incredulous.

I was, I suppose, also pleased in a sense that I was not alone in my misery, that I was not unique among congressional wives. Misery loves company, I suppose. But any comfort I felt was mitigated by sadness at the extent of the corruption in Congress that corrupted marriages, at knowing that for so many women in Washington the party had long been over.

Four

"Walk a Mile
in My Shoes"

"Join Congress and see the world!" the advertisement should read. "You will be spirited to exotic, faraway areas of the globe, and it will not cost you one penny. The American taxpayer will pick up the tab. And don't worry about running short of cash. Your friendly military attaché will be there with a ready supply. A sumptuous meal awaits you as you and your wife board your specially equipped air force luxury Boeing 707. If you're lucky, you might even get LBJ's old presidential jet.

"You will not have to go through customs, wait in line anywhere, or deal with the mundane chore of transporting your luggage. There is a military crew to take care of all these boring details."

There were at least ten congressional junkets to choose from during the Christmas break in 1977. John and I chose a trip led by New York Cong. Lester L. Wolff that was investigating drug trafficking throughout the world. Wolff was known to work members of his groups hard, but John decided to go, anyway.

We were picked up at our home by one of those boatlike, shiny black cars stamped "U.S. Government" on the side in gold letters. At Andrews Air Force Base, a shiny blue and silver Boeing 707 with "United States of America" stamped on its side was waiting. We were ushered into a lounge and served hors d'oeuvres and drinks.

As on other official junkets, an air force official called out each couple's name when we boarded the plane. They seated us according to congressional seniority. Since John was only a one-termer, we were seated toward the back. But on air force planes, all seats are like first class on commercial flights. And, as on first class elsewhere, personnel—in this case military—make sure you are well fed and that your every whim is satisfied.

We stopped at Alaska to refuel—not only the plane, but its passengers. In the officers club at the airport, greeted by our top military brass, we were served lobster, shrimp, Iranian caviar, and cocktails. It was obvious that the military wife led as regimented a life as congressmen's wives. There she was, forced to stand in this club, entertaining total strangers and smiling all the time while her officer-husband tried to impress the visiting congressmen. This scene was to be repeated many times over the next three weeks of my "travels with John." In each country, we were wined and dined royally by the American ambassador, his wife, embassy personnel, and the leaders of the host country.

Every so often, John and I departed from the official itinerary. In New Guinea, ignoring the protests of our terrified driver, we headed off into the bush. John spotted an aborigine village that we had to walk for miles to reach; I trudged along after him in my little congressman's wife outfit, an uncontroversial suit with shoes to match.

The villagers surrounded me and began to touch my blonde hair. This particular Clairol product is a unusual shade for New Guinea. John was laughing so hard that tears came to his eyes. I was standing there preoccupied with thoughts of what had happened to Rockefeller in New Guinea. We traded pieces of clothing and food for a water jug, a hand-carved whistle, a fertility statue, and a handmade axe. (Later, we would donate many of the pieces to museums in South Carolina and Texas. The Smithsonian asked us for two of the pieces.)

Our tour covered Tokyo, Canberra, Kuala Lumpur, Singapore, Bangkok, New Delhi, Teheran, and Dublin.

In Bangkok, Lester Wolff was placed under tight security since the Thai drug community was said to have placed him on its hit list. This made sightseeing logistically difficult for everyone.

I passed up lunch with the other wives and a DEA (Drug Enforcement Agency) agent took me to a jewelry shop where I bought six rings for very little money. A few of the other wives, miffed at having missed out on the jewelry bonanza, were cool to me for the rest of the trip.

One of the wives, however, became a good friend of mine—Ann Badham, wife of Cong. Bob Badham of Newport Beach, California. We developed an immediate rapport, and we shopped together, swam together, and really enjoyed each other's company. But I think that we both knew that our friendship was limited to this trip. We could never continue upon our return to Washington. Bob was a Republican and as far right as one could be. He represented a wealthy suburban district. And John, of course, was a liberal Democrat representing a district that contains two of the poorest counties in the United States. The knowledge that politics would stand in the way of any lasting friendship with this woman I liked so much cast a pall over the entire trip.

I was shaken, too, by our experience in Manila. President and Mrs. Marcos entertained us lavishly. When we arrived at the palace, the men met with the president, and we met with Mrs. Marcos. She was wearing a blue Adolfo suit and Gucci shoes, with pave diamonds encircling her neck. Her nails were perfectly manicured, sculptured-looking. Every hair was in place in an upswept French twist.

Mrs. Marcos is, of course, more than merely the first lady of the Philippines. She is the second most powerful political figure (if not the first?), with a multitude of government titles.

Although she conveys great femininity, she also displays a strength beyond anything I had ever seen. It showed in her eyes, in her voice, this practically indescribable determination and ambition.

Her sitting room was appointed with exquisite European antiques. She sat at the head of the room in a large, regal-looking chair covered in velvet. On her right and on her left, we congressional wives were arranged according to our husbands' seniority, more or less flanking Mrs. Marcos. And over on the left side of the room, apart from our group, were the wives of her husband's political allies.

Mrs. Marcos spoke of her country and what she had done for this country she loves, the cultural center she had just completed with her money and the kinds of programs she was trying to institute for her people. She referred to the people of the Philippines as her "children."

We then joined the men for lunch. During lunch, a TV set was wheeled in, and we watched a videotape of the country's celebration of Marcos's rise to power.

When we arrived back at our hotel, gifts awaited everyone. The more senior the congressman, the more opulent the gifts for him and his wife. I received a pearl-encrusted jewelry box, and John, an inlaid pearl chess set with hand-carved wooden chessmen. In addition, the wives in our group received Filipino clothing, hats, and baskets with crafts, shells, and jewelry in them.

Beyond the banquets, beyond the palace, the poverty of the people was startling. Sometimes, talking to people in the streets, you'd mention the Marcoses, and they'd look terror stricken. Our stop in the Philippines was a sobering experience.

Father's Day in 1978 was one of those times when John and I were secluded in our home creating the illusion that we were just a normal couple spending a day together. We had the phone receiver off the hook. When I finally put the receiver back on the hook, the phone rang. It was my mother, crying. She hadn't been able to get through to me; she'd been calling for hours. My brother-in-law Brad, was in the hospital in critical condition. He had gone that Father's Day to Oklahoma City to buy some horses —his hobby was raising horses. I assumed that he had been in an automobile accident, but it seemed that he had been hospitalized, instead, with severe stomach cramps. Doctors had performed an emergency operation. Brad had a malignant tumor, a rare form of cancer that the doctors said was incurable.

My sister, Gladys, didn't accept the prognosis. I didn't accept it, either. Brad was the healthiest person I knew, physically and mentally. He was more like a brother to me than an in-law. During my first marriage, he had been my lifeline. At other times, when I was doing impulsive, nonthinking sorts of things, he would be right there to give me advice and guide me. My sister was always there for me, too. They were two people I could always count on, and I think their ability to be so supportive of me derived from the strength they gave each other.

They had been sweethearts in high school and college. They got married right after college, and their marriage was somewhat of a miracle, in my experience. They had two small daughters, Stacey and Ginger, and Gladys was expecting their third child at the time Brad became ill.

I went to Texas to see Brad that June, and he looked fine. He was a very handsome man, tall and rugged-looking. He had been an All-American basketball player, and he had kept himself in shape. He never drank or smoked; he taught a Sunday school class in Hurst, Texas, where he and my sister lived. He was almost too good to be true, just invincibly normal—and, I thought, invincible.

When I saw Brad again that Christmas, I knew he was dying. I had brought him a gift that meant a lot to him, a lovely Kaiser China horse from Germany. I had bought the horse on a junket that turned into the only honeymoon John and I ever had. Instead of returning to the United States with the congressional group, I talked John into buying Eurailpasses and traveling through Germany, Austria, Italy and Spain, taking with us only extra pairs of jeans, toothbrushes, and my fur coat. We slept on the trains, using the coat as a blanket.

I tried to penetrate the wall of pain and resignation that separated Brad from me, from all of us, with chatter about my idyllic, crazy weeks of being just plain Mrs. Jenrette in Europe. I explained to Brad the diet that Dick Gregory had recommended for him. Dick had also told me what vitamins Brad should take; I had brought lots of vitamins with me.

I now know, and I think I knew then, that nutritional remedies were not going to help. But the chemotherapy treatments were not helping, either. At the time, we were all ready to try anything. Brad would have tried anything to be saved; this went without saying. Brad never talked about dying, not even with my sister. That Christmas, he and I talked when he was feeling well enough, and I wanted to tell him that I knew he wouldn't be with us much longer and to try to comfort him and comfort myself. But I didn't know how to say it, and that added to my sadness then and does now because I know those moments, that conversation, would have been important to me. As it was, I was helpless, unable to be a real support to the man who had been more supportive of me than anyone in my life.

In January 1979, I began having to cope with another, different kind of trauma. My husband requested that the Justice Department conduct an investigation of his business dealings following allegations that he was involved in a drug-smuggling operation with Johnny Etheridge, in Darlington County, South Carolina.

Johnny Etheridge was the chairman of the Democratic party in Darlington County, South Carolina. He was also Jimmy Carter's and John Jenrette's campaign manager in that area.

Johnny is a very hyperactive individual. I intuitively felt something was wrong with Johnny and Pam (his wife). During the 1976 campaign, Johnny and Pam devoted a 100 percent effort toward John's reelection, but in 1978 things had changed. Johnny had hoped to run for John's congressional seat. John had promised Johnny that he would take on Strom Thurmond in 1978. But Pug Ravenel had already announced his candidacy for Strom's seat, and this dissuaded John from running.

Etheridge was caught in January 1979 smuggling marijuana into the United States from South America. The plane was found to be loaded with several million dollars' worth of marijuana at the Darlington airport when confiscated.

Etheridge began to sing like a canary. The "sled" agent, who had worked undercover on this case, had tapes of Etheridge implicating John, the state attorney general, Tom Liden, and a U.S. senator.

John asked Att. Gen. Griffin Bell to investigate the charges. Nine long months later, Etheridge admitted he had lied about John's involvement in the drug-smuggling ordeal. I thought our ordeal was over, but it had just begun.

John and I were in Myrtle Beach on the weekend of January 18.

That evening, my mother called and said she didn't think Brad would survive the night. John didn't want to fly to Houston with me, but I insisted. We left immediately. A highway patrolman drove us at about 120 miles an hour from Myrtle Beach to Charleston. John started drinking the minute we got on the plane; I suppose he was unable to deal with the enormity of the situation, with my pain. He started going from seat to seat, shaking hands with the passengers and saying, "Hi, I'm Congressman John Jenrette." Then he started making wisecracks. "Let's take this plane to the Bahamas and thaw out the stewardesses."

A young man with a beard came up to John; he was wearing blue jeans. He looked like a student. He asked John if I was his wife, and John replied, "Yeah. Can't you see the ring in my nose?"

The man with the beard came over to me, looking concerned. I guess my misery was obvious to everyone. I was afraid we wouldn't get to Houston in time. I was wrestling with the whole awesome, awful concept of Brad's dying at all. The bearded man asked me what I ever did to deserve "a husband like that."

"I don't know," I said.

Then another concerned passenger, a tall, stocky businessman type, started talking with me. "Is your husband really a congressman?" he asked.

"Yes, he is."

The man shook his head. "I'm really sorry he's acting like that," he said. John, at this point, was flirting with the stewardesses, putting his arms around them, even pinching them. I poured my heart out to the businessman, who had sat down next to me. I told this perfect stranger about Brad's dying. A perfect stranger, merely by serving as a sympathetic listener, offered the comfort that my husband withheld.

And then John walked up to us and said, "Hey, buddy. You can look at her, but you can't touch her."

"Well," the businessman said, "if you'd be a little more compassionate, maybe some stranger wouldn't have to sit down and comfort her at a time like this." He and John almost got into a fight.

After we landed in Houston, I could no longer control my resentment of John. "You've been acting like a complete ass," I told him. "I need you. I need your arm to lean on, and you haven't been there for me."

"Well, I'll turn right around and go back to Myrtle Beach," John said. "I don't need to take this. I didn't say anything wrong. You can't even take a joke. So what if I said, 'You see this ring through my nose?' Or so what if I was talking to the stewardesses? Really, you're so temperamental and jealous, I can't believe it."

I was almost in tears; I couldn't talk anymore.

But John was a different person when we reached the hospital, when we entered Brad's room. He was just as grief-stricken as I was. Maybe his behavior on the plane had been his own way of coping with emotions that he couldn't or didn't want to face.

But there was no avoiding reality now. It was five o'clock in the morning. Brad was burning with fever, slipping in and out of consciousness. John helped me fan him and put ice on him.

Eventually, we checked into the Holiday Inn across from the hospital to take a brief nap, we hadn't slept for twenty-four hours. We were awakened by the ringing phone—a nurse from the hospital. Brad was dead.

We found my sister sitting on the hospital bed holding Brad in her arms. He had a sweet smile on his face. Everyone had been trying to get my sister to leave, but she wouldn't let go of him. I hugged her, and she said, "He really loved you so much," and we hugged, and I was so filled with pain that I couldn't cry. And we all stood around—Brad's parents and my sister and John and me. We just stood there immobile, as though suspended in time. And there was sweet Brad lying there with a smile on his face. And it was over. It was really over.

Finally, my sister went to tell Stacey and Ginger. Ginger didn't understand what had happened; she was only three years old. But Stacey was nine, and she did understand. She was crying uncontrollably. I was holding her and telling her that her daddy was in heaven now, and he was in pain, but he feels so much better now, and all the while I knew that my words couldn't comfort her over the loss of her father. It's a pain that can't be ended, really. You just have to somehow live through it.

We went back to Brad's parents' house, into the room where Brad had been staying only three days before. And there was his American Express receipt from having flown on Southwest Airlines from Dallas to Houston with his signature "Brad Brown." Only ten days before, he had flown there, and he was alive. There were his shoes standing where he had left them and his billfold with pictures of my sister and Stacey and Ginger and the new baby, Brad, Jr., who had been born only five weeks before. There were all the mementos from his childhood, his basketball pictures, and his basketball. There was his whole life in this room, and he had been there only three days ago with his shoes and his pants and his coat. And now he was no longer of this world.

My sister asked me to deliver the eulogy at Brad's funeral. I remember sitting up in the pulpit with the minister and praying that I could get through it. The church was packed. I remember that my mother was the last person to come down the aisle, and she was carrying little Brad, the baby, and she was trying not to cry. I thought, "Dear God, if you can help me get through this, I can get through anything."

So I didn't look at my mother or my sister or anyone; I focused somewhere above all the peoples' heads, and I read what I had written from my heart the night before:

"Brad had a strong sense of who he was and set high moral standards for himself. Yet he did not judge others by his own yardstick. He allowed the people whom he loved and who loved him to be themselves without being judgmental of their choices.

"Brad died as he lived, with strength and dignity and concern for others. The day he died, he was mentally alert and continued to comfort each member of his family. When the doctor told him he had little time to live, he said, 'Doctor, I'm not afraid to die, but I have an awful lot of people whom I love, and I want to live.' He said God had blessed him in so many, many ways and asked God to give his angel, Gladys, the strength to go on living if he were to die.

"I have never seen the type of strength that Brad showed all of us that day. I know his life and death taught those of us who loved him how to live and how to die. Brad will never be forgotten, and Brad will always be a part of those who loved him."

I finished reading, and I sat down, drained.

Brad was buried on a hill overlooking a pasture with the horses that he loved, and from his grave you can almost see the house he loved so much where Gladys and their three children still live.

During the months following Brad's death, I learned that what is even harder than death of someone you love is living with the knowledge that that person—in this case, my true lifeline—is no longer there. When I needed John during this lonely time, he was not there, either. It seemed as if he couldn't grasp the profundity of my sorrow. If I tried to talk to him, he'd run away.

I kept hearing rumors of his infidelities; I kept trying to convince myself these were just rumors, which, in the gossip-mongering Washington environment, was not difficult. In fact, that beautiful "honeymoon" train trip through Europe led to a rumor with such staying power that I would not hear about it until the Abscam trial was underway, when a reporter came up to me and said, "Well, I heard about the time that you flew back from Europe alone after a junket because you had caught John in the arms of another woman."

In the context of Washington, practically anything John told me by way of explaining why he had not come home until four A.M. sounded plausible to me.

Then, too, his drinking was an excuse. "He was intoxicated," I'd tell myself. "How could he get home? Or course, he had to spend the night at ———'s house."

I couldn't easily explain away the phone calls from strange women, in one instance, a stewardess who told me, "Congressman Jenrette promised to pick me up at the airport"; on another occasion, I picked up the phone to overhear a woman's voice inviting him to the Indianapolis 500, and I was so furious that I smashed a priceless statue from New Guinea.

I was constantly at war within myself, my reasoning powers combating my intuition, my knowledge of John's past and present errant behavior constantly casting doubt on my image of him as I hoped he was and wanted him to be.

During Congress's Easter break in 1979, John and I joined a congressional trip to South America. It became obvious, during lavish receptions in Quito, Lima, and Rio, that John's drinking had increased to an enormous extent. In Lima, John came down with the flu. The navy physician assigned to this trip was an extremely good looking thirty-eight-year-old colonel. He came to our room to treat John, and he was very kind—in fact, too kind. He cornered me in the hallway. I pushed his arm away and walked back into the room, determined not to make a big deal out of the incident.

The next day, John had to fly back to South Carolina to attend a Democratic political function. His first-class flight was paid for—by the taxpayers, ultimately—but we were unable to afford my plane fare, which would have come out of our pockets. So I had to stay on the tour in order to return on the official, free flight.

Rio! The whole city throbs with energy, passion. My suite faced the beach; the view was spectacular. What a setting for romance, for a torrid affair. I had a candidate, too. The handsome navy doctor was pursuing me with renewed ardor now that John had left. And I was tempted. John's infidelities and continued drunkenness had begun to take their toll.

I looked up an old classmate of mine who had married a Brazilian. Ellen and I had been friends for twelve years. I went to her lovely home, and she, her husband Byron, and I spent the evening reminiscing in a room filled with photographs of her famous grandfather, John Foster Dulles, and President Eisenhower; it was like a retrospective of American politics in the fifties. Ellen was quite distressed about a book that had been written about her grandfather. The book was the main topic of conversation.

Later that evening, the navy doctor joined us at Regine's, a disco as electric as Rio itself. Although I had invited the doctor along, his presence soon began to make me feel uncomfortable. He wanted me. I could feel it and see it in his eyes more and more, and I felt myself responding, too.

I asked Ellen to drive me back to the hotel—quickly—because I did not trust myself to return alone with the doctor to our hotel.

I locked myself in my room and ran to the balcony. I took deep breaths as I looked out over the ocean shore far below. I longed for someone to share all this beauty with. John had not fulfilled my needs, physically or in any other way, for such a long time. But I couldn't bring myself to be unfaithful to him. I couldn't view an affair or the possibility of one as something I could or even should do—for myself. Having an affair was being unfaithful to John. I'm not a player; it's not my style. Even in Rio, I couldn't let myself go.

The phone kept ringing. There was repeated knocking on my door. I didn't pick up the phone, and I didn't open the door. I knew it was the doctor. If I let him in or even talked to him, I thought, I would be defenseless, totally vulnerable.

The next day, as our congressional group was preparing to leave Rio, I noticed some of my fellow travelers nudging one another and smiling in my direction, but the smiles were not friendly; they were judgmental. I knew that everyone believed I had slept with the doctor. As I took my seat on the air force jet to return to the States and to John, the doctor sat down next to me and placed his hand on my arm possessively. I yanked my arm away. The little scenario did not go unnoticed by the members of the group. I comforted myself. *Well, I know I'm innocent. If others want to fictionalize my life, that's their problem. I'm not guilty; they're presumptuous.*

I rationalized and rationalized, but it didn't make me feel better. I appeared to others as the original fallen woman. In a way, I wished that as long as I was to have this image, I had lived up to it, really lived it up. But I hadn't. I had lost the moment.

And I was a fallen woman, in a way, but not in the traditional sense. I was falling into a chronically depressed state, because of John's infidelities, his drinking, his lies, the stories that conflicted with his staff's stories—he didn't even bother to synchronize what he told his staff about his whereabouts with what he told me—and his staff's hostility. I thought, from time to time, that I was being paranoid about

77

his staff, overly sensitive about things like their not sending me flowers or even condolences when Brad died. But another congressional wife confided to me feelings similar to mine. She was older, a veteran. "You'd better get used to it," she said when I asked her if her husband's staff was hostile to her. "They consider you a pain to be dealt with. And they want to trot you out like a Barbie doll when it's time for you to put on your little suit and your little smile. But then, when they don't need you, they would prefer that you just fade away."

I had become so immersed in John's life, in the Washington political life-style. I was addicted to it like a junkie waiting for a fix. It was enough just to keep up. I didn't have time to question what was happening to me. I had lost my ability to function independently. The staff told me where to go and what to do, and if I had balked before or questioned their plans, now I waited for their instructions. I soon found it hard to get out of bed in the morning. I would lie in bed most of the day. Sometimes I managed to go jogging—I wanted to clear my head —but the positive periods didn't last very long. I would call my friends Bob Rose and Linda LoPresti in New York, two musicians I had met through friends who were in the Starland Vocal Band. Bob and Linda are the sanest people I know, with a relationship as solid as Brad's and Gladys' had been. I confided in Linda and Bob completely. They listened to me recount the latest bizarre event in my bizarre life, and they tried to get me to connect to their world where love and loyalty went hand in hand. They were my anchor, giving me a realistic perspective on the poisoned glitter of Washington that I couldn't seem to escape, even with their help. But I didn't want to escape. I loved John. I made

RITA JENRETTE
MY CAPITOL SECRETS

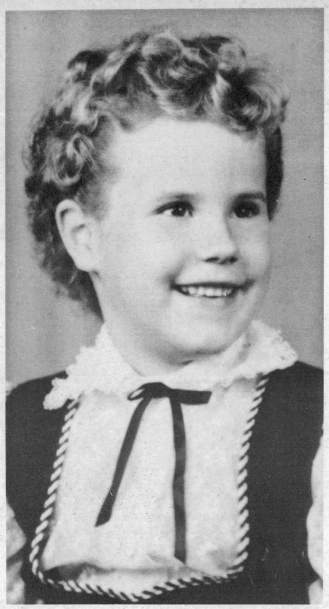
Rita Carpenter, at age 2.

Rita, at age 11.

Senior year graduation
from St. Mary's Academy
in Austin, 1967.

September 1979, with John and Bob Hope
at a reception in the Kennedy Center
for Hope's new movie "The Road to China."

Rita consoling John after his conviction
on charges of conspiracy and bribery
stemming from the FBI's Abscam investigation,
October 7, 1980.
(UNITED PRESS INTERNATIONAL)

Phil Donahue listens with the audience and
8 million American viewers as John calls Rita
live on television to tell her of his alleged
embarrassment at Rita's posing in *Playboy*.
(WIDE WORLD PHOTOS)

Rita taking a break from reporters' questions
at a press reception at New York's "21" Club.
(WIDE WORLD PHOTOS)

One of Rita's *Playboy* poses. (WIDE WORLD PHOTOS)

that clear to Linda and Bob. They would tell me later that they found my loyalty to him unbelievable. I called them every time John had done something crazy, something hurtful, and I'd ask them, "Isn't that crazy?"

And they'd agree that it was. They thought my life was bizarre, and it was. But no sooner had I poured out the awful event—I suspected that John had been unfaithful or John had been drunk and behaved disgracefully—than I would start defending John to Linda and Bob. He had been unfaithful because he was drunk. He had gotten drunk because he couldn't take the pressure of the federal investigation of his conduct.

During the summer of 1979, John and I were invited by the governor of one of the states to spend a secluded week together in his private compound on a Caribbean island, just us and his bodyguards—until the governor flew in by helicopter with his eight-year-old daughter. He was a very handsome man, I thought, a Rossano Brazzi type, and very fond of John. John had done a great favor for him through his committee work.

We went for a cruise on the governor's yacht. While John was on the upper deck entertaining the governor's little daughter, I relaxed below, half sprawled on a deck chair in my string bikini and coverup, getting some sun. Suddenly, I felt someone's foot grinding into my toes. Startled, I opened my eyes and saw the governor standing over me, laughing, and sticking out his tongue at me in a suggestive way. I sat up, clutching my coverup, and frowned and stared away at the shore in the distance.

John waved at me from the deck above. I made a

frantic signal with my head as if to say, "Get down here this minute." John misinterpreted the signal and waved again.

When it was time to go back to dry land, the governor swan dived off the boat and swam ashore. John followed, diving from the upper deck—he had had a few drinks—and belly flopped. When the governor's daughter and I got into the little dinghy provided for us, I was so nervous I capsized the boat, and we landed in the water, too. Fortunately, the sharks that had been reported recently in the area were nowhere to be seen. But it wasn't really the sharks I was worried about.

When we all went for a walk a little later, the governor—unbeknownst to John—kept clutching at my rear end. Then, as I was taking a shower, there was a knock at the bathroom door.

"John?" I said.

A male voice answered, "Yes." But it was not John. I pulled the shower curtain around me, and the governor pulled me to him, ripping down the shower curtain. "Rita, Rita," he said.

"Later, later."

He left the bathroom, probably encouraged, although he should have gathered by then that what I meant was "Never, never."

That night, the governor set up a dinner on the beach. It was overwhelmingly romantic—the lovely table, moonlight, the surf pounding in. And there I was with a lecherous host and a drunken husband. Both of them ended up with their heads in their plates.

Three weeks later, back in Washington, the governor called. I picked up the phone and immediately recognized his voice, murmuring my name.

"Would you like to speak to John?" I asked. "He's right here."

By August, the federal agents had added two more charges to the drug-trafficking charge against John: They alleged that John was involved in payroll kickbacks and had filed phony travel vouchers.

Bob and Linda were my refuge from my own life, which had become hell on earth. They tried to humor me back to myself. I'd arrive at their apartment to visit, and I'd come in the door with my politician's wife's smile pasted on, as if John's staff had just wound me up and I was on automatic pilot, greeting the voters. And Bob and Linda would say, "Okay, cool it. The cameras aren't rolling. The press isn't here. It's just us, your friends Bob and Linda. You can stop being Mrs. Jenrette now. You can be Rita." Bob joked that he was thinking of getting a chair shaped like an open convertible, just for me, so I would feel at home when I visited!

But when Bob and Linda weren't around, when I wasn't on the phone with them, I would lose my perspective, lose control on my own life to John's frenetic political life-style and our personal melodrama in which my role became more and more that of his protector. We'd go to South Carolina so that he could make a speech. He'd get drunk, and I'd put him to bed and go make the speech for him. I'd lie and tell people that he had been delayed in Washington on congressional business or that his plane was late. I covered for him maybe ten times, maybe twenty—I lost track. On one occasion, when President Carter sent Hamilton Jordan to South Carolina, I went to the function and covered for John.

And I remember, one time during the summer of 1979, when we were in South Carolina, staying at the Howard Johnson's Motor Lodge in Myrtle Beach, and I stood on the balcony of our top-floor room, maybe seventeen stories above the ground, and I thought, *It would be so easy to jump—and*

*then I wouldn't have to deal with any of this, any-
more.*

When John went to the Schick Center, Richland
Hills, Texas, outside of Dallas, an aversion-therapy
clinic, in October to try and treat his alcoholism, I
was, at first, optimistic. He had been to the Schick
Center three times before. Maybe this time he
would beat his alcoholism. What I didn't know was
that John, a brandy drinker, had told the doctors
that he drank Scotch. He was going down there and,
through his treatment, developing an aversion to
Scotch.

And he also was carrying on with a staff member
at the center. I didn't know that, either. But when I
found out, when the evidence had mounted to the
point that even I could no longer overlook it, I would
have rented a Lear jet just to catch him with her,
because every time I had confronted him with evidence of something like this, he had convinced me I
was wrong, jealous, paranoid, possessive, and I
would end up blaming myself, thinking that I was
losing my mind. As it turned out, I took a commercial flight to Dallas to see for myself what was going
on.

I first suspected that John was getting more than
therapy for his drinking problem at the Schick Center when he stayed at the Capitol several hours
after Congress had adjourned the night before he
was to leave for one of his trips to Dallas. This, in
itself, was not unusual. But when I tried to use his
office WATS line from our home, it was constantly
busy. And I thought he was talking to someone and
didn't want me to know, or else he could have made
the call, or calls, from our home, which he often did.
I was furious. Who else would stay at the Capitol
until two in the morning? But I kept my anger to
myself.

The next day, as I drove him to Baltimore-Washington Airport to catch the Texas International plane to Dallas, he picked a fight with me in the car. He was yelling and carrying on about trivia.

Usually, I went with John to his rehabilitation sessions in Dallas, but he had decided we couldn't afford this extravagance anymore. So I put him on the plane, and I tried to put my misgivings behind me. I had developed a new philosophy, something like I'm okay, he's okay—or at least we were going to be fine once his drinking stopped, once the Justice Department investigation of him was over, once I stopped questioning John's integrity and that of his fellow legislators and stopped resenting protocol and managed to become the perfect politician's wife.

I was constantly developing a new philosophy more or less along these lines. And every time I developed one, John would do something to sabotage it and whatever vestiges of self-esteem I had left.

At around eight o'clock the night John left for Dallas, I decided to call him. I wanted to tell him that I loved him and to say, "Thank you for going back to the center. I'm glad you're doing this for yourself. I know it'll work." But mainly I just wanted to hear his voice.

So I called the Schick Center. I was told, "Your husband doesn't answer his page."

I said, "But you nurses only have thirty people or so down there. You know where every one of them is all the time because you have to keep an eye on them. I don't like this."

The head nurse got on the phone. "Oh, Mrs. Jenrette," she said, "your husband called and said he won't be in until midnight."

"What do you mean? His plane arrived at five."

"Well, he called and said he wouldn't be in till midnight."

"Okay, fine. Thank you."

I had asked my sister Gladys to meet John at the airport with a box of candy—for moral support. So I assumed he had gone to her house for dinner.

I called my sister and asked how she and the kids were, then, "How's John doing?"

"Well," she said, "All right, I guess."

"What do you mean you *guess?* You mean he's not there?"

"No, Rita. I don't quite know how to tell you this. I'm sure there's nothing to it." Gladys had met John at the airport; he had known she was going to meet him. He even knew she would bring him a box of candy. And Gladys had said, "I'll take you over to the Schick Center." John had told her, no, that they had sent someone to pick him up. And he had introduced my sister to a woman who sounded, from Gladys' description, like the staff member at the Schick Center.

I called the center again and unleashed my rage at the unfortunate person who picked up the phone. I said that "one of your staff members is having an affair with my husband, and it's unethical and unprofessional."

I was told that no employee of the center would ever go out with a patient.

"Well, one of them just has!" I said, nearly choking on the words.

I slammed down the phone, and all I could think of was renting a Lear jet. I had to get to Dallas immediately. I had to see, right now, that my husband was really with another woman.

I got on the phone and called National Airport; there were no jets for rent that night, Lear or otherwise.

It was five A.M. when I went to the airport and

boarded a plane for Dallas that stopped in Chicago. When I arrived in Dallas, exhausted from pent-up rage and lack of sleep, I went to the Schick Center, straight to John's room. He was in the bathroom, throwing up—the immediate result of aversion therapy. I said, "Good, I'm glad you feel sick. How could you come down here and screw around? How could you? With an employee here?"

A nurse ran in and told me to get out. "He's doing his therapy!"

"Fuck off!" I said, as surprised at my behavior as she was. I had always been so concerned about people liking me. Before I married John and after I married John, I had gone out of my way to be nice to everyone, pleasant, because it was so important that everyone like me. My musician friend Bob Rose once called me "the most well-behaved person he ever met," and this was not exactly a compliment; he thought it was somewhat abnormal to be so well-behaved. He meant I was a doormat.

So here I was, all of a sudden, telling this nurse, "Fuck off! Get out of here! We're paying for this, and I'll come in here if I damn well please. Furthermore, I have a lot of friends in the press, and if one of your employees went out with my husband, I'll damn well have it put in the papers. Because you're exploiting alcoholics."

The staff member was fired. And, eventually, I felt sorry that she had been fired. Why shouldn't she have gone out with this handsome, charming congressman? How many opportunities did she have to go out with a congressman, after all? John was more at fault than she was. She was single. He was married.

I told John later, "Listen, why don't you just paint a penis on your pants? Then everyone will know you have one."

My thirtieth birthday, November 25, 1979, was a shambles. John and I were in Myrtle Beach having a quiet dinner alone. The phone rang. I answered it. It was a local politico, a big Jenrette supporter, who said John just had to help him out with his election that evening. I explained that it was my birthday and we were celebrating with a dinner alone, together. The politico told me a plane was on its way to pick John up and that he'd be back in a very short time.

John didn't return until two A.M..

He was as much a slave to his constituents as I was to him despite my bursts of lucidity, my fighting moments, my short-lived vows of "I'm not taking any more of this."

Our lives had become a soap opera. I would probably have regarded the scenario as ludicrous if I hadn't been playing one of the leading roles.

In November 1979, three months before the soap opera was aired coast to coast, with Abscam, I took one of John's constituents out to lunch. This woman had come to Washington with her daughter, and before she left, she finagled John into paying their hotel bill. He paid, too—$400. That's how far constituents' demands can go—and for all I know, they can go farther. Naturally, I was called upon to play gracious hostess to this woman and her daughter.

Over lunch, she said to me. "You're so lucky to be married to John."

I had heard that line before. But this time I thought, *Why doesn't she say how lucky he is? Why is everyone always telling me how lucky I am. Why doesn't anyone say how lucky he is to be married to someone who loves him enough to lose her identity over him?*

I brought the woman and her daughter back to

our house, and we opened the door and smelled gas. The oven door was open, and there was a TV dinner inside, still in its carton. John had turned the gas on, but the pilot light was off. The fumes were pouring out, but the smell was faint in the living room. John was passed out on the couch with the phone receiver to his ear, but the line was dead.

"Has he been drinking?" the horrified constituent asked.

"Yeah," I said.

I eventually managed to wake John up after getting my uninvited guests out of the house. We stayed awake for the next twenty-four hours together. John had to go to South Carolina to testify again in one of the various hearings that had plagued his life for the past year.

The Schick therapy had failed, but I didn't mention his drinking that day or the following day. I knew how upset he was about testifying again. I thought, *Everyone's after him.* I thought he was guiltless. And the Justice Department, as it turned out, thought so, too—at least for the time being.

Five
Abscammed!

On November 26, 1979, the day after my thirtieth birthday, John and I were back in Washington, although he knew he had to return to South Carolina two days later to testify at the Billy Lowe trial in Columbia. The thought depressed him utterly.

Billy Lowe, in my opinion, is an innocent victim of the insidious nature of politics. Lowe is a Darlington businessman, an honest, hardworking family man. He was the foreman of the grand jury looking into John's alleged involvement in selling underwater lots. When Johnny Etheridge arranged a meeting between John, Billy Lowe, and Robert Floyd, Lowe attended the meeting—innocently, I believe, as he had attended so many political meetings before. Yet when Etheridge was caught in the marijuana-smuggling scheme, he put the finger on Lowe, Rob, and John. Lowe was the fall guy.

I stayed up all night with John on November 26, comforting him. At around seven A.M., I left for a one-hour jog at my gym. When I arrived back at the house an hour and a half later, John was nowhere to be found. The front door was wide open, and leaving the door open is something one does not do on Capitol Hill.

My head began reeling. *Is John walking around*

nude? Should I call the police? No, I can't. Will he be picked up for inderent exposure? As I looked out our bedroom window, I saw a woman walk down the steps to our basement apartment, which we rented to another congressman.

I threw off my jogging suit and put on a dress. I combed my hair and walked briskly down to the basement. When I opened the door, there lay John, completely drunk. Across from him sat the woman. I extended my hand to her and said, "Hi, I'm Rita Jenrette."

She was clearly shocked. "Oh, my name is Nancy," she said. "I work for the congressman that rents this apartment. He's flying in today and asked me to pick up some papers for him." She walked to the back of the apartment as if she were familiar with the place.

I called Diane Robinson, a trusted member of John's staff, and asked her to come over. Diane helped me carry John up to our bedroom. Doug P. Wendell, John's administrative assistant, helped me get John into the shower. I rushed downstairs to the kitchen and put a steak in the microwave oven. Doug put John into bed, and I hand fed John his steak. We then let him sleep for a few hours—we had to catch a plane to South Carolina!

By noon, we were on the private plane, as scheduled. I turned to John and said, "Who is that woman I found you with downstairs?"

"I've never seen her before in my life," he said.

"If you're lying, I'll never trust you again."

"I swear," he said, "I'm telling you the truth."

We arrived in Columbia, South Carolina, and spent the night going over John's testimony with Alex Sanders, Billy Lowe's attorney.

The next day, I drove to Myrtle Beach to check Nancy out. It turned out that she did not work for the congressman who lived in our basement apartment. She worked for a Texas member of Congress. She had met John while he served on the appropriations committee.

I called Nancy and said, "Hi, this is Rita Jenrette. I want to know what you have going with my husband."

She was flabbergasted. "Oh," she stammered, "Mrs. Jenrette... John has showed me a side of Washington I've never seen before. I'm going through a terrible divorce, and John has been my best friend. He has helped me so much."

It took every ounce of strength I had to keep from screaming. All I could think was, *Where was my husband when I needed comfort and support after Brad's death? All those nights I sat with dinner getting cold and crying myself to sleep—where was John then?*

Once again, John talked his way out of this situation. I actually found myself apologizing to him for doubting his sincerity!

In December 1979, a man named John R. Stowe began visiting our home in Washington on a daily basis. Stowe, a native of John's home town, Myrtle Beach, South Carolina, had moved to Richmond, Virginia, and now wanted to return to the beach. He had found a factory, American Gear & Pinion in Conway, South Carolina, that was in bankruptcy. He also had a "finance man" to back his regeneration of the factory. He wanted my husband's help in securing the loan.

This was not an unusual request for a congressman to receive. Lobbyists, constituents, and just people in general enjoy flaunting the fact that they know a legislator personally. I've never deluded myself into thinking that the majority of these people, whether they are favor seekers or just status conscious, truly cared about John as a person, much less about me. They wanted John around because he was a congressman. They wanted me because I was a congressman's wife. This awareness always helped me in keeping at least some small perspective while living in Washington, with its towering façade of power. I say "façade" because I am talking about that power that exists in the minds of people who are attracted to the powerful, the people I call "the lurkers."

Stowe was a power seeker, anxious for my husband to impress his "financial people" whom John met for the first time at a house on W Street. By the end of January 1980, when Stowe told John, over lunch, that he had enlisted Strom Thurmond's support for the factory in Conway that would provide jobs for five hundred South Carolinians, my husband was becoming rather tired of dealing with Stowe. He felt that he had done all he could do for this constituent.

All that I knew about John Stowe during December and January was that he would come to our house and take my husband out and my husband would come home totally intoxicated. After one such occasion, I told Stowe how much I resented his dragging John off like that into an environment where he felt free to drink himself into a stupor.

It wasn't until that awful Saturday afternoon, February 2, 1980, that I learned more about John Stowe. I listened, horrified, to the FBI agents' questioning of my husband. John Stowe's "financial people" had been FBI agents posing as representatives of Arab sheiks (who didn't exist). The mythical sheiks were supposedly interested in backing Stowe's South Carolina factory. In addition, the fictitious sheiks wanted Cong. John Jenrette to introduce legislation that would enable them to stay in the United States. For this, they offered to pay my husband $50,000. And the FBI told John on February 2 that they could prove that he had accepted the bribe, that they had his dealings in the house on W Street on videotape.

February 2 was a busy day for the FBI. They had leaked word to the press that they were closing in on eight Washington politicians who were suspected of accepting payoffs for political favors. They were winding up their Abscam investigation, which had begun in 1978. Tom Snyder and *New York Times* reporters, among others, had the whole story. So the FBI spent February 2 notifying seven Congressmen, including John, before the media broke the news to the general public.

All my life, I had kept diaries. Writing down events and my thoughts and feelings about them was as cathartic for me as jogging. As of February 2, I began keeping a nearly daily record of the drama that was building around me not only as a means of diffusing the increasing pressures on my psyche but also because someday, I might want to have a straight accounting of the facts and my feelings. I wanted to keep notes to help prove John's innocence. My memory ten or twenty years from now might replay the months after Abscam in soft focus or out of focus. So I wrote everything down as it happened, and the following excerpts from my diaries are the clearest picture I could give:

Saturday, February 2, 1980

After the FBI agents left, the long vigil with an aide and our lawyer lasted until the early hours of the morning. John and I were in shock. Tom Snyder knew more about our predicament than we did. The major networks arrived on our porch and would not leave. The phones rang continually.

Jack Vardaman, our lawyer, had told me not to speak with any reporters. I said that I didn't agree with him. By and large, in this town, I've found the press to be the most real or substantial people around. I said that I thought John and I should be honest, to the point, and open. Everyone else thought that we should keep silent because our words might be twisted.

Left alone at last, John and I embraced in a silence and agony I will never forget. We fell into bed, clothes and all, too numb to talk and too emotionally drained to sleep.

Sunday, February 3, 1980

The phones began ringing at eight A.M. The TV cameras were still outside. I got up, got dressed, and decided to go to church. I thought that if anyone could help us, God could. The network cameras followed me down the block. I chatted briefly and honestly with the reporters.

My neighbor walked with me to St. Marks. I said a prayer for John with the members of the congregation, some of whom stared at me. I knew that they knew our situation, and I felt uncomfortable. I thought, *Get used to this, kiddo!*

Mike Fernandez, John's campaign manager, a person we had grown close to in a very short time, came over at one P.M. He climbed over our back fence to avoid the TV cameras.

Mike agreed with me that John had nothing to hide and should address the network reporters. As John was getting dressed, Mike and I discussed John's political future. It was dismal, but I knew it would take John some time to reach this painful conclusion. He had worked all his life for his office, and controversial as he may be, he was and is a good congressman.

Throughout the day, John, Mike, and I digested the facts as we knew them:

1. John was introduced to Abscam by Stowe, who had a legitimate constituent request.
2. John did not receive $50,000, as the FBI alleged.
3. John did borrow $10,000 from Stowe but signed a note. (Thank goodness!)
4. John himself admitted his two occasions on W Street were spent drinking, and heaven only knows what he said on tape while in an intoxicated state.

Clearly, he admitted he bragged about his power, etc. But due to his drinking on the two occasions, he did not have any idea of what he said or did not say. This, of course, does not look good. However, at least he did not take any money.

Tuesday, February 5

We got up early. John, as usual, went down to get the *Washington Post* in the buff. It is always by the door, and he merely hides himself as he reaches out for it.

This morning, the *Post* was a bit farther down the porch. John peeked out our curtain and saw no one. He rushed out to pick up the paper, and the cameramen filmed him in the nude. We laughed for the first time since Saturday.

I laughingly told John's aide about the nude incident. They became extremely upset.

I talked to the camera crew, who said they would not use the footage.

A member of John's staff called and suggested that we not drive our old Mercedes: "It might look bad to the people in the district." I said, "We are who we are. We cannot be something that we're not. How can you tell us not to drive our own car?"

More calls, more press, more TV cameras.

At 6:15, I received a call that John (who was spending the afternoon at his office) was drinking. Lord knows, if anyone had a reason to drink, he did. I rushed to his office, picked him up, and we went to Germaine's, our favorite restaurant. I thought it would cheer him up. Instead, he was recognized. He put his head in his hands, silently expressing the outrage and hurt he was feeling. His life, as he has created it, was crumbling before his very eyes. I felt at a loss for anything to say or do to comfort him.

We drove home in silence, each hurting for the other.

A call from Warren Clayton, our press secretary. A New York newspaper has been leaked info from the FBI that Stowe is an informant.

John called Stowe. I recorded the conversation, and it clearly absolves John. Of course, this is not admissible in court.

John seems to be taking everything out on me at the moment, but this is understandable. He is particularly emotional tonight, and who wouldn't be?

Wednesday, February 6

Not wanting to wake up but knowing we had to, that we had to face another confusing day, John and I pulled ourselves out of what had been at best a troubled sleep. The doorbell was ringing, and we both looked at each other, wondering if the press was still camped outside our door.

We glanced out the window and saw two friendly faces—our campaign coordinators Marvin Chernoff and Mike Fernandez. Marvin has been a good friend for many years, a man whom we deeply respected. He flew from Columbia, South Carolina, earlier this morning to be with John and me.

Marvin and Mike wanted to gently break to John their feelings concerning his political future. They both felt John's life as a congressman was over regardless of the results of this Abscam farce.

To be completely candid, I, in a sense, want John and me out of this insane political life-style, continually living out of a suitcase, never knowing whether he will have a job from year to year. A politician's job is based on the whim of constituents. And they think he's responsible for any thing that affects their lives. If the price of gasoline goes up, their congressman is at fault. If their taxes go up, their congressman is at fault.

Certainly, Congress has its share of scoundrels, but it has its share of statesmen, too. Congress represents our society as a whole and is no better or worse than the American public as a whole.

This seems to be John's most painful and difficult day so far. I hurt with him but seem to be unable to comfort him. It's not easy to comfort a person whose life has become something undefined.

Thursday, February 7

I met with two press friends of mine and told them that I had recorded a conversation between Stowe and John that seemed to clear John of the FBI allegations. But one of the reporters snatched my enthusiasm away by shooting immediate holes in my defense of John.

John is good and decent but truly a misunderstood person. How can I explain this to the skeptical reporters?

Saturday, February 9

I am so angry at John's staff that I could scream. They influenced him to go to the district and make two speeches this weekend. I cannot believe their callousness toward John's personal well-being. We have been through perhaps the most trying week of his life, and he needed this weekend to pull himself together and rest. Yet his staff convinced him that he needs to attend two major meetings in South Carolina. It is sheer stupidity.

I am pulled in two directions. One, I want to be with John if he needs me. On the other hand, I'm so furious with his staff that I want no part of what are their plans for the weekend.

CBS just called. They'll be filming John at his first stop in Georgetown, South Carolina. I pray he can keep himself composed.

Monday, February 11, 1980

John left at ten A.M. to meet with Jack Vardaman, our lawyer at the Williams firm. Stowe is to be at the meeting. Hopefully, he will clear John. However, if Stowe pocketed the $50,000, then he will be reticent in clearing John.

Yesterday, I watched "Agronsky and Company" and felt contempt for one or two of the reporters who were taking a sanctimonious approach to the Abscam ordeal. The lone female of the group stated that she knew of many members of Congress who would have turned down an invitation to the W Street house. This is a damned exaggeration. I know of no member who would not go to a home in Georgetown at the request of a constituent to discuss employment in his district. In fact, I've seen members of "Agronsky and Company" at parties in Georgetown.

George F. Wills, whom I seldom agree with, was much more objective. He felt that the FBI leaks were reprehensible and might ruin the reputations of innocent people.

Yesterday, in the *Post*, I read that John was alleged to have seen the $50,000 but did not take the money. Why are people assuming that he received the money? I don't understand it. Or perhaps I understand the mood of the press and the people as a whole all too well. It is an ugly mood, a mood that seeks to blame the ills of the country on the elected official.

I just heard Carl Rowan giving his opinion of the Abscam trap. He was so condescending and sanctimonious. I immediately called CBS and stated my objections to Rowan's commentary defending the FBI's entrapment of congressmen. I think the woman who answered Rowan's line was a bit stunned by my polemics.

It seems as if I'm furious with many, many people right now. I wonder if I'll ever be the same again.

Last week, on Thursday night, a constituent called from John's home-town area. John had just fallen asleep. The constituent was drunk and asked me if I really loved John or just married him for the status of being married to a member of Congress. He asked me if I would stay by John through this crisis. A total stranger calling out of nowhere questioning my character and most personal feelings! But he was a constituent, a supporter of John's. I felt I had to suffer through his obnoxious innuendoes and inferences.

I'm still constantly amazed that people feel they can interrupt our evenings, our dinner, our leisure time, basically the little time John has away from his congressional work.

A man called one time regarding a tobacco matter, and I said John was eating his dinner. The man became irrate and said that either John could come to the phone or lose his vote. As John picked up the phone, I thought, *What price a vote?*

Thursday, February 14

I woke up at 2:30 A.M., 3:30 A.M., and now it is four A.M. and I am unable to sleep. I didn't enter any thoughts here yesterday because I was unable to think straight.

At two P.M. yesterday, FBI agents entered my husband's congressional office. They were serving subpoenas to staff members. It seems the grand jury will begin hearing evidence against John on February 28.

Two of John's staffers are leaving his office for greener pastures. One is his administrative assistant.

I've been devoting the majority of my time to compiling information to assist John in his defense effort. Last night, I went over his telephone log and appointment book. It was interesting to note that Stowe contacted John last March (1979) in an effort to get his son into one of the military academies. Prior to this time, John had not seen Stowe for years.

Beginning in August, Stowe accelerated his calls to one to three times a week, as documented by John's call sheet, the last call occurring on January 30, 1980.

I certainly recall Stowe calling our home almost nightly from November until a few weeks ago. He was also coming by our home and dining with us. I did not care for him at all. This guy was extremely nervous and on edge. I voiced my opinion to John.

However, I frequently become agitated when people try to monopolize my husband. And it was not unusual for constituents to monopolize John's time as Stowe was doing or for me to voice my qualms about such people.

Stowe had even tracked us down in Texas over the Christmas holidays.

We have also learned that on the Saturday that the FBI infested our home, Stowe was chatting with the FBI for three hours at their headquarters. My perceptions of this man were right on target.

Tonight we have to fly to Nashville; John is making a speech to a tourism group. I really dread going. We will, of course, be expected to attend receptions, shake hands, and endure the inevitable stares that accompany the Abscam press-induced recognition. If I don't go, people will speculate that we're having marital trouble. I can't deal with that type of gossip at the moment.

Of course, I'm certain this ordeal is taking its toll on our relationship. It is impossible to describe the type of pressure we're experiencing, the sleeplessness, the confusion, the anger, the frustration. I almost feel as though we are actors in some sort of soap opera. I keep hoping I'll wake up and this will all have been a bad dream, but I know that won't happen. This is reality. And it's hard to digest much less comprehend and accept.

My emotions can't catch up with the events.

Friday, February 15

John finally arrived home late yesterday afternoon, a bit—rather, quite a bit—tipsy but in time to catch the plane to Nashville.

Just before we left for the airport, a network friend of mine called to deliver some bad news: the Justice Department intends to pursue Kelly's and John's cases posthaste. Their grand jury inquiries—or, at least, John's—will begin on the twenty-eighth of February.

One thing comes to my mind: are they using John (a little fish) as a trial case, or do they have a good case against him?

John slept on the way to Nashville as I anxiously mulled over the news of his impending trial. All I could think of was how tired I was and how tired John was, and here we were on a plane to Nashville, having to paste on the old political smile for the group John was to speak to. How I longed to be home, just he and I. Instead, we were facing one more strange hotel room.

The press was waiting for John. Cameras were rolling. Bleary-eyed, John gave them a thirty-minute interview. I knew he shouldn't be doing this because of his exhaustion, and, indeed, he did make a few unwise statements. Who wouldn't?

We got to bed at midnight. I slept until eleven A.M. this morning because I really needed the rest, but I missed John's speech, and that made me feel guilty.

When we arrived home tonight, John's staff informed him that a major political supporter of his had died. We were told that we must fly down to South Carolina and attend the funeral. Of course, I have to go, or the press will speculate that I'm going to leave John. Just this week, a UPI reporter called and said that it was rumored in South Carolina that I would be leaving him. Can you imagine? Don't I deserve my own life? After all, John's the congressman; I am his wife. Can't I miss a function every so often without the rumor mill anticipating our imminent demise?

Saturday, February 16

Elizabeth, John's seventeen-year-old daughter, arrives this afternoon. I love her very much, but I hope she manages to tone down the hostility she sometimes directs at her dad. I know this is expected of a child who lives with one parent and sees the other infrequently. But I am not in a state of mind to act as the peacemaker today.

We picked up Elizabeth and her friend at the airport, and she seemed genuinely happy to see us. I can only hope that this experience will show her there is an exciting world outside of North Myrtle Beach, South Carolina. Elizabeth has tended to reject opportunities we've tried to offer her.

When I took her to commercial-shooting sessions with me for Clairol in New York and for Breck in Atlanta, she acted extremely bored even when the agency man showed interest in using her as a model. I tried to take her to a play in New York, but she just wanted to find a Wendy's hamburger place! But she's only seventeen.

Sunday, February 17

For the first time in ages, I talked John into jogging with me. We jogged five miles, all around the Capitol. It was a glorious day, absolutely beautiful.

We both felt extremely good. This day was ours to spend as we chose, that is, until the early evening when we received a call from a constituent and a staff member asking if we could travel to South Carolina a day earlier than the funeral itself. That means leaving tomorrow. It seems that they're having a political meeting to choose a new leader to replace the man who died. It's a must that John attend. Or so they say.

I haven't decided if I'll go with John tomorrow. I know I'd be stuck in a motel or in a friend's home waiting for him to return from nightly political meetings. At least in Washington I have transportation, friends, and things I need and can accomplish. On the other hand, if I don't go, it will appear as though I'm not being the supportive political wife.

Monday, February 18

Today—rather, this evening—I flew with John to South Carolina. He had been drinking heavily, and we had an argument on the plane before it took off in front of all the passengers, many of whom recognized us. I was embarrassed and almost got off the plane. However, I sat down instead and hoped John would sleep—which he did.

Tuesday, February 19

John had to make a speech at the funeral, which he did quite well. I was amused that a woman who, according to John's administrative assistant, had once had an affair with John showed up at the funeral. I went out of my way to greet her. "I've heard so much about you," I said. She seemed shocked at my direct attitude.

The funeral took up much of the day, and John had to stay out until three A.M. working with the local politicos. I don't know how much longer he can keep up this pace.

I talked with the Washington office, and the staff was fairly upset. Three men had walked into John's office, one dressed in a long Arab gown; one with a camera; and one in a three-piece suit. They were from one of those tabloids, trying to set up a fake picture for their paper. They gave our secretary a false phone number. I can't believe we're experiencing this type of harassment!

Wednesday, February 20

We were preparing to catch a plane back to Washington, and John learned his staff had arranged a meeting with five farmers—at the airport!

John has just read the inaccuracies Stowe was putting out in the press. He was quite upset during the drive to the airport. He slept most of the way back to Washington. I was struck by how troubled he appeared to be. He was falling apart before my very eyes. The false accusations and innuendoes were destroying him, and there seemed to be nothing I could do. I feel helpless and impotent.

Thursday, February 21

Today I met with my minister. He really listened to me. I hardly gave him a chance to talk. I suppose I was overflowing with a need to express my feelings.

In a strange way, I felt as if I were betraying

John by unloading my problems on our minister. As a rule, John would have served as my sounding board. Now it is impossible for us to communicate fully. Things are just too confusing.

When I arrived home, John's daughter brought her friends over for Cokes and snacks. Her attitude has become very positive. I am elated!

This evening, the same constituent who called and asked if I really loved John, if I hadn't really married him for his position, etc., called again with the same harangue. I became very upset and hung up on him.

I called John and asked him to get in touch with this man and tell him never to call our house again.

The man called a second time.

I picked John up at his office, and as we walked in the door of the house, the phone was ringing. It was the sick constituent again.

I'm having our phone number changed.

Friday, February 22

I called a friend in South Carolina tonight. She was not home, but her sister answered the phone. She said she had to get something off her chest. She wanted me to know that she had slept with my husband. She said she had felt guilty every time she had seen me at her sister's home, and she wanted to "set the record straight." She said the affair took place before John and I were married.

I kept silently asking myself why she felt guilty or compelled to confess to me if the affair took place before our marriage.

I slept very little even though I had run three miles that evening. All I could think of was what my friend's sister had said.

Saturday, February 23

Four political leaders from South Carolina came to our home this morning to implore John to run once again for his congressional seat. They said they were behind him 100 percent. I suppose he will run even if it kills him.

I left the meeting to pick up Elizabeth for lunch. We returned home to find John intoxicated. I put him to bed and took Elizabeth and her friend shopping. When we came back, John had gotten up and was feeling much better. However, he took another drink and began getting drunk again.

It's as if he wants to stay oblivious to his troubles. I guess I might feel the same way if I were in his place. Nevertheless, it's very difficult for me to keep everything together.

I don't know if I can take this.

Sunday, February 24

Elizabeth left for South Carolina this morning. At 1:30 P.M., John had a staff meeting to reorganize his office after the departure of his administrative assistant.

The four remaining staffers seem genuinely concerned about John. Perhaps I've misjudged some of his employees.

Richard Davis, John's political operative, showed me an editorial in a South Carolina newspaper. It called for John's resignation. I immediately sent off a letter to the editor in support of my husband. Whatever happened to due process of law?

Friday night, my closest friend among the congressional wives called to say that she's left her husband. I'm truly saddened. This is my third friend in the last six months who's divorcing a member of Congress.

It is not so much the man each of these women is leaving but the way of life and what they have become. In a very real way, I envy the freedom my friend has gained, to be herself, to dress as she pleases, to regain control of her life, to be rid of the groupies and the pressure and the intrusions into one's privacy. I've forgotten what it's like to go somewhere and to be with someone because I want to and not because I am sent a schedule that politically charts our moment-to-moment existence.

Monday, February 25

The staff picked up John this morning at six A.M. They were flying to South Carolina for a Communications Workers of America (CWA) meeting.

John arrived back this evening at six P.M., totally exhausted. He was in bed trying to rest when a staffer called and said he had to get up and make an important vote.

Tomorrow the grand jury starts hearing evidence against John. This is so difficult to live through.

John's press secretary was a bit upset with the letter I wrote to the South Carolina newspaper defending John. He advised me that it would be better for John if I kept my feelings to myself. What do they think I am made of?

Thursday, February 28

John was torn between going to South Carolina and staying in Washington to make twenty votes scheduled to come up on the floor of the House. He missed his first plane and decided he wanted to stay with me in Washington. However, his administrative assistant became very upset and insisted that John catch a later flight to the district. Bone tired and weary, John made his commitment.

I flew to New York to be with Bob Rose and Linda LoPresti. I had to spend time with people who cared about me, the human being—not me, the congressman's wife.

I think the trip is going to help renew my energy and perspective.

Friday, February 29

I flew back to Washington to be with John, who also flew in today. We're both exhausted and in much need of rest.

Saturday, March 1

Today is my dad's birthday, and in all the confusion I forgot about it. I called my dad, who was most understanding.

John slept much of the day.

It snowed at least a foot. The snow was quite beautiful.

Monday, March 3

John's secretary called this morning to say that she had received a call from Ed DeHart concerning the RIAA annual dinner. Mr. DeHart wanted us to avoid embarrassment and not go to the dinner because the FBI would be receiving an award from the recording industry.

I hit the roof. I called Mr. DeHart's office and told his secretary how appalling it was that the FBI would be receiving an award from the recording industry, my area of work!

Apparently, DeHart then called John's office,

and John's staffers were most exasperated by my candor.

Tuesday, March 4

Today I spent some time on myself, getting my hair, nails, etc., done. It felt good to pamper myself a bit.

At 4:30 P.M., I met with my "shrink", who is really being a great help.

At six P.M., I picked up John, and we went to a marriage counselor. The meeting seemed to be productive.

Later, we met John's campaign coordinator at Germaine's restaurant. Marvin is still contending that it would be better if John would decide not to run for Congress again.

John is fighting the negative political forecasts "tooth and nail." I know he will run regardless of how the political climate is in his district. I certainly sympathize with his not wanting to accept the changes that are so quickly transforming his life.

Thursday, March 6

I was sick today and stayed in bed most of the day.

I did hear some good news concerning my last Nashville recordings. A recording lawyer, David Ludwicke, is pushing my tunes.

I suppose when it rains, it pours. I've been waiting for a career break for such a long time, and now it comes in the midst of this Abscam mess. Life is ironic, to say the least.

Monday, March 10

I suppose I am getting reticent about even writ-

ing my thoughts and feelings in this book anymore.

Thursday, March 13

Where do I begin to recount this rather mind-
boggling week?

It began with John flying down to South Carolina and back on Sunday and ended with him ad-
mitting himself to Bethesda Naval Alcoholic
Rehabilitation Center on Wednesday night.

I knew things were getting bad on Tuesday
when John arrived home drunk and incoherent.
We were scheduled to have dinner with a lobbyist
and his wife. I really didn't know what to do. I put
John to bed and went to the dinner. I said something about John's having contracted the flu.

But last night was the "icing on the cake."
John got up yesterday morning (Wednesday) and
felt he had lost the entire day of Tuesday. I was
incredulous. Obviously, his drinking had reached
an acute stage.

He left the house to meet with our lawyer Jack
Vardaman.

I left for my spa to run. When I returned, I
found John sitting in the kitchen sobbing. He told
me that when he had arrived at Vardaman's, Williams and five other lawyers had joined the group.
Williams told John that the fees for his defense
would be $200,000.

In addition, they told John that he should plea
bargain with Justice. John was distraught. He
said he hadn't taken any money. He wasn't guilty.
Yes, he got drunk, and he doesn't know what he
said on the Abscam tape, but *he did not* accept
any bribe money.

I can't even imagine the horror John must have

felt when Williams laid this bomb on him. How could Williams pull the rug so abruptly out from under a man under the kind of pressure John is enduring?

I had an appointment with my therapist, and John insisted that I go. I reluctantly left after asking John's new administrative assistant, John Miles, to come over. I had never seen John in such an emotional turmoil.

I rushed home following my session and found John totally drunk and threatening suicide.

I panicked. I asked John whom I could call that he would talk to. He said Rick Nolan, a wonderful congressman from Minnesota; Rick came over, and he and I begged John to enter Bethesda for treatment. Finally, John agreed.

It was a horrifying night.

Saturday, March 15

Yesterday and today proved to be the most trying days as yet. I was sleeping yesterday morning when a reporter knocked at our door. My big mistake was in talking to him at all. He convinced me that he was a person one could trust, etc. What an ass I was! The man took everything I said off the record and much I never said and depicted my husband as a suicidal nut. I couldn't believe it.

After meeting with this reporter, I did something even more disastrous. I called Benjamin Civiletti and proceeded to give whoever answered the phone a piece of my mind.

It's so hard to sit silently by as you watch people unjustly destroying your husband. I can't seem to control my impulse to tell people exactly what I think of them even though by doing so I might be playing right into John's enemies' hands.

Today the bomb hit with the horrendous and misleading article about John.

I am so very depressed. I'm at fault. They twisted the truth, and I feel responsible. I really don't blame John's staff or friends for being furious with me. My intentions were good, but I said too much, and much of what I said was misinterpreted.

Perhaps I should write a book on *Four Easy Ways to Lose Your Husband's Congressional Seat.*

I am leaving tomorrow for Myrtle Beach and Florence, South Carolina, to represent John at various political functions. It's going to be difficult.

Sunday, March 16

I drove out to Bethesda to see John before I hit the campaign trail. He seemed preoccupied, and I felt as if I were getting on his nerves.

The staff put me on a flight to Florence rather than Myrtle Beach. We felt this would confuse a certain reporter who was going to try and trail me around the district.

In general, people down here seem a bit nervous in my presence, as though they hardly know what to say to me. Tonight at least the crowd was friendly. Tomorrow will be something else.

The staff and I are getting along well. We have a common purpose now—survival.

Monday, March 17

It is midnight, and I have been traveling since five A.M. I have given a speech introducing the consul general from Canada, Ralph W. Stewart, in Florence; a TV interview; a press interview; a Rotary luncheon speech in Myrtle Beach; a live radio interview. I rode in a parade; had dinner with the consul general and his wife Suzanne; and was driven for two hours back to Florence.

The reception was mixed today, with most people reacting initially as though shocked by my presence.

Tomorrow will be much the same. You know, I realized something about myself today. I can receive five positive responses to John and one negative one, and the negative response stands out. I am still not tough enough, I suppose. The negative people always affect me.

A reporter from Washington came down to cover my campaigning. The staff doesn't like him and decided I shouldn't speak with him. The newsman became irate and finally left. I suppose he'll write a terrible article about me.

I felt foolish in the parade, riding alone without John.

Tuesday, March 18

I was picked up at eight A.M. by staffers to donate prized art objects that John and I collected in Papua, New Guinea, to the Florence Museum (South Carolina).

The film crew arrived, and the newspapers reported the event. I think it is surprising to John's staff that I'm receiving positive publicity. Actually, it surprises me a bit, too.

Yesterday at the Rotary Club appearance in Myrtle Beach, a senior citizen was pinning a rose on my jacket, and we were having a delightful conversation. She told me her name, and I told her mine. At that point, her face fell. She and her friends seemed dismayed that they had actually enjoyed chatting with John Jenrette's wife—as if they expected some ogre.

It's hard to be in Myrtle Beach, John's home town, where his ex-wife still lives. Today, following the museum visit, I had lunch with John's campaign director, then toured a black beauty school John had secured funds for.

Then I was driven to Myrtle Beach by our tax attorney. We stopped in Aynor to chat with one of my favorite people, Mayor Hoyt Johnson. We stopped at his drive-in liquor store just in time to see my early-morning interview on the television. I watched myself, drank a Coke, and felt as if I were doing a good job for John.

Wednesday, March 19

I woke up this morning in strange surroundings once again. It's really difficult living out of a suitcase. It never feels quite right sleeping in a strange bed. It seems that due to my great success, the staff would like me to stay down here through the weekend.

I ran a few miles, which made me feel better.

I had to M.C. a fashion show in North Myrtle Beach. As I glanced over the crowd, some six hundred people, I felt the hostility I had anticipated. I wanted to do well, particularly since the woman who was coordinating the event stated that so many of the women were coming just to see me "fall on my face."

As it turned out, a page of prepared lines were deleted from the program without informing me, and I was introducing the wrong names for the people modeling various outfits. It was a fiasco.

One good thing, though. My stepdaughter Elizabeth was there and gave me a wonderful introduction. It made me feel very close to her.

That night, until about 2:30 A.M. our tax attorney and I conferred, trying to figure out what we could sell to pay the Williams firm their legal fee. Damned if I know where we're going to get $200,000.

Thursday, March 20

I went to Conway to pick up some money that one of John's friends had owed him for years. It would help pay our lawyers. The man was elusive. I finally tracked him down in Aynor and got the check from him.

I then drove back to Myrtle Beach and worked with several of John's associates on selling some of our property. We had to have the money to pay the lawyers.

Friday, March 21

I'm so exhausted, but I must go on. In Johnsonville, I got the mayor's unofficial endorsement of John. I visited Wellman Industries, our biggest supporter. Billy Mace, Jack Wellman's right-hand man, says Jack is reluctant to give John a fund raiser. I said, "We need him now, not later." Billy says I should see Wellman personally in ten days.

It is quite humiliating to grovel before people, begging for contributions.

Hemmingway, South Carolina: a press bit; a radio spot; a well-attended meeting of black supporters in Kingstree. I'm glad I agreed to speak here. Some of John's opponents showed up. I think my speech was inspired!

Saturday, March 22

I got to bed at two A.M. last night. This morning, I was up at seven, drove to Dillon, South Carolina, to give a speech to the Young Democrats. I got a standing ovation. Then home to D.C.

Sunday, March 23

I slept, jogged a mile, and drove out to see John at Bethesda. I had missed him. Our roles seem to have changed temporarily. He was waiting for me to call while *I* was on the campaign trail. What a switch!

Monday, March 24

Calls and more calls. I am deluged by calls from John's staff, friends, and family. I'm feeling so strong now. I could take a bit less strength.

I paid John's lawyer $7,000. He said there was little hope John would not go to prison. I was so depressed when I left his office.

Tuesday, April 22

The last few weeks have been hectic, to say the least. I have been campaigning from five A.M. until midnight in John's district. After four years, John's staff has finally begun to see me as a valuable asset. Isn't that ironic?

Last week, I attended sessions at Bethesda with John. He seems to be changing in a very real way. He is growing spiritually and is developing more sensitivity. He gave a very thoughtful interview to Lee Bandy (of *The State* newspaper). Lee told me he had never written such a candid personality piece. Yet John's detractors claim his new involvement is a political hype. Sometimes this life makes one quite bitter about human nature.

If this ordeal had to happen to bring about

John's spiritual and emotional growth, then I am thankful for it all.

Our lawyer says John will be indicted between May 15 and June 1. Charming. Just ten days before the primary.

I'm not saying John is an angel, but he's not the crook Justice is presenting to the country. He's a good person. He had an acute drinking problem. They used him at his most vulnerable point.

Friday, May 2

After six weeks in the alcoholic rehabilitation center, John departed last Friday for South Carolina, spent one night in our home in Washington, and is back in South Carolina again. Truthfully, I feel quite neglected.

Yesterday I worked on my music with Margo Chapman and John Carroll of the Starland Vocal Band. We are scheduled to work again today. I will not give up this time.

The group therapy at Bethesda that I am attending each morning has been very good for me; the group is very supportive. They see a value in me and a potential. They listened to my latest recording and said it would be a great sin not to pursue my singing career—much-needed encouragement.

Through the group, I have seen how I have been making John's staff (who, in general, dislike me), the lobbyists (who couldn't care less about me), and John's friends a major part of my life. I have put myself in a situation where I could expect little positive feedback and much criticism.

When I told the group that John treated me much better than most political wives are treated by their spouses, they were appalled.

Sunday, May 4

It is 11:20 A.M., and I am on the plane back to Washington. I flew down to South Carolina yesterday afternoon to steal a few hours with John. However, it didn't work out that way. A man who had driven John to the airport to pick me up thrust an article in my face that quoted John as saying that his two hobbies were drinking and sex. I threw the article on the floor of the car. I wished I had never bothered to come. Had I bothered to read the article, I would have seen John's statement as a reflection of his past behavior rather than current behavior. I had to ponder what kind of pleasure the constituent got out of thrusting the quote in my face in the first place; it was more his problem than mine, I guess.

I had overreacted. I was really unfair to John. The incident reflects how very low my self-esteem is at this time.

We finally arrived at our friends' guest house where we generally stay in Myrtle Beach. We had only been there for fifteen minutes when our hostess, her children, and a few other people came over. I suppose no one understands our need to be alone. I wanted and needed to have John to myself, particularly after the incident in the car. I dropped hint after hint, but it didn't seem to register with the visitors. When we finally had an hour to ourselves, we locked the doors, got undressed, and began to make love. However, we were interrupted by two knocks on the door and three phone calls.

At 5:30 P.M., John's staffers picked us up, and we were at an NAACP meeting until one A.M. When we arrived back at the guest house, John's son was lying on our bed. So much for being alone.

Sunday, May 25

Campaigning and more campaigning. We started out at nine A.M. today. John and I attended four church services, two white and two black. It was quite an enjoyable experience. In fact, rather joyful.

The first service was held out in the country, a rather charismatic event. The Baptist minister talked with John and me alone in his office. He asked me if I knew God and if I accept Christ as my savior. I said, "Yes." Then he asked John if he had accepted God into his heart.

John replied that he was trying to but didn't know how to do it. The pastor then read several passages from the Book of Romans to John. He asked John if he was ready to be born again. John said, "Yes." John repeated a passage after the minister and began to cry.

I was so moved. I know this sounds corny, but it was very real.

Tuesday, May 27

I am once again on Flight 14 from Myrtle Beach, South Carolina, back to Washington, D.C. John had a five A.M. plant gate and spent the night in Florence. Once again, we are apart.

If the wife of a Jenrette opponent would spend one day campaigning with me, she would see what she'd be in for as a congressman's wife: loneliness, struggle for identity, neglect.

Thursday, May 29, 1:53 P.M.

My loving husband just called me from Myrtle

Beach, South Carolina. He was a bit curt and hurried. He was on his way to yet another late-night campaign stop. Actually, I have doubts about his late-night campaigning. I know him so well. I wish I couldn't see through him.

Today I was reading a quote from Joan Kennedy stating how her husband's infidelities caused her to doubt her attractiveness, her intelligence, etc. I certainly can relate to that!

Wednesday, June 11

John's primary was held yesterday, and he is now in a runoff with Hicks Harwell, a flamboyant politician. Yesterday, as we waited for the election returns, I ran a few miles. It was a virtual madhouse around our hotel room, aides running in and out, photographers shooting pictures, reporters vying for interviews. Around eleven P.M., we realized John had received 48 percent of the vote, and we had to go to headquarters. The crowd chanted "Jen-rette Jen-rette" as we walked in.

I eventually became tired of being elbowed out of the way and sat outside headquarters by myself.

The phone rang all night in our hotel room. We finally slept a little between five A.M. and nine A.M.

I got up and jogged with John, which seemed to alleviate the tension.

Today we filed an $11 million lawsuit against Civiletti, Weingarten, Kotelly, Webster, etc. We do deserve compensation for the harassment inflicted on us by the Justice Department.

I jogged again this evening at nine P.M. when we arrived in Myrtle Beach, hoping to unwind. However, I find it difficult to relax.

Johnny Harrelson, chairman of the Democratic party in Darlington, called at 10:30 P.M. and requested that I meet a plant gate at five A.M. (Georgetown Steel). I suppose I will meet the gate.

I find it so demeaning to beg people for their votes. I really wonder what John gets out of this.

Friday, June 13

I've never been superstitious until today. Friday the thirteenth. At 1:45 P.M., John was indicted on three charges, one on conspiracy and two on bribery. I feel like shit!

At four P.M., we arrived at the Ramada Inn in Florence for John's press conference on the indictment. Three of John's opponents' supporters showed up wearing Hicks Harwell buttons. It made me furious.

Driving back to the hotel, I held John as he quietly sobbed. There was little I could say or had a need to say. The silence was broken only by the sound of our car bumping along the road.

As we walked into our room, John grabbed me, and I held him tightly in my arms. I told him I love him regardless of the outcome of his trial.

I suppose the reality of this situation is that John must go to jail. The primary runoff is almost irrelevant now. John is at this moment meeting with his political advisers about where to go now politically.

I don't find my thoughts flowing at this time. I feel uptight, queasy, numb.

Whenever thoughts of my own career come to mind, I push them away to a future place, knowing the impossibility of pursuing anything now.

I must say, as I read the indictment, I was shocked. I don't know what I expected, but I didn't expect the contents of the Justice Department's press release.

It is almost the same feeling I had when my brother-in-law died. You are prepared for the death, yet when it comes, it is totally devastating.

Six

Guilty?

As you can see from my diary entries, I believed in John and in his innocence. But as 1980 progressed, I, once John's greatest supporter, began to have more and more doubts. Still, I wanted so much to believe.

The summer of 1980, after John's primary victory and his indictment, was one of great tension, anticipating his upcoming trial (to begin the first week of September).

We spent most of August working with Kenny Robinson, the lawyer, who was now handling John's defense, preparing for the trial. One day in Kenny's office, John was admiring the Rolex watch that another of Kenny's clients was wearing. John struck up a conversation with his client, a jovial-looking man with a round, red face and twinkling eyes.

John had a presidential solid-gold Rolex that I bought him the previous Christmas and had just paid off. Yet this man's Rolex had a different band and a different face, and John wanted one just like it.

The man with the Rolex that John suddenly coveted was an ex-CIA agent, Frank Terpil, who would later flee the United States, evading indictment on gunrunning.

John and Frank Terpil became fast friends. A few days later, Terpil showed up at our home. John told me they were going out to lunch to discuss trading watches. I thought, *Well, if one week before your Abscam trial all you can think of is Rolex watches, so be it.*

As I watched Terpil and John climb into the chauffeured, New York-tagged Mercedes, my heart sank. I thought, *John is up to something, and it means trouble.*

The next day, Terpil called at around eight A.M. He assumed that John had filled me in on his Idi Amin idea. I calmly acted as though I knew what he was talking about. But a little voice in my head was shouting, *Idi Amin?*

The plot unfolded. Terpil was close to Idi Amin. Idi Amin was close to the Ayatollah Khomeini. John and Terpil felt that if they could talk Idi Amin into persuading the Ayatollah into freeing the fifty-two American hostages in Iran, then John would be pardoned by President Carter since all of America would view them as heroes.

Believe it or not, the idea did not seem that farfetched at the time. I had experienced some pretty strange things as John Jenrette's wife.

I called *Washington Post* columnist Rudolph J. "Rudy" Maxa and asked him to meet John, Terpil, and me in Kenny Robinson's office. We all listened as Frank dialed direct on Kenny's line to Saudi Arabia, to the penthouse suite in the Hilton Hotel in Jedda where Amin was staying.

Kenny later said the call cost him $125.

Terpil kept saying, "Amin, your excellency." And

Amin was saying, "I'll help you, my friend, but only if the congressman can get my children in U.S. schools."

John got on the line and said, certainly, he could place Amin's children in school. He asked Amin how many children he had. Amin responded that he had thirty-eight children. John almost dropped the phone.

Frank Terpil later laughingly explained that whenever Amin saw a beautiful woman, her husband would disappear, and Amin would take her as his wife and adopt her children.

There would be numerous phone calls to Idi Amin —and one to Andrew Young in Atlanta. When Young returned John's call, I listened on an extension phone. John said, "I talked to Idi Amin, and he said he could get the hostages released into his custody."

"Listen," Young said, "I'd rather that the Ayatollah have the hostages than Idi Amin."

That evening, Terpil popped up on our doorstep with his beautiful girl friend, Cyra. I was finally figuring out that Frank Terpil was not merely an ex-CIA agent. I said, "Frank, why is Kenny your lawyer?"

"Oh," he responded, "they're charging me with murder in New York. They say I killed someone for Quaddafi." He said all of this with a twinkle in his eye.

I choked on my Diet Dr. Pepper. In fact, I spilled my drink all over the rug. I excused myself to go to the bathroom, still choking and coughing.

Locking the door of the bathroom behind me, I sat down on a little French chair. I looked in the mirror and said out loud, "I have a suspected murderer in my home." I considered sneaking out the back door and driving away. "Oh, no," I told myself, "I can't leave John in there." All of this for a new Rolex watch?

I nervously returned to the living room. Cyra was just saying that America's leaders should be bumped off. I actually felt faint.

Then Terpil proceeded to tell us about an agent friend of his who gets a thrill from breaking into peoples' houses and "blowing them away." Terpil proceeded to go to our front door, look outside both ways, and then he and Cyra were gone like a puff of smoke.

I said, "John, I know I told you I wanted to make some new friends, but—"

The next day, a man named Jack Morris, who's from Myrtle Beach, flew into town. He was going to be one of John's trial witnesses.

John, Jack Morris (who could barely walk because of his injuries), and I were driving from a meeting with Kenny Robinson back to our home when John suddenly announced that we were going to visit Frank Terpil in his mansion directly across the street from Ethel Kennedy's home, Hickory Hill, in McLean, Virginia. I said, "John, I don't feel well at all, and I would like you to drop me off—"

"No," John said, "I want you to go. I want to see Frank's home."

We argued, but John was driving, so I told myself to be calm. What could happen across from Hickory Hill?

Frank Terpil's home was a magnificent Japanese-style mansion, the likes of which no CIA salary could ever pay for. It had secret passage ways and a firing range in the basement. Terpil said that whenever the FBI boys drove up, he'd just pop inside a wall. When he added that he had quite a few enemies who would like to see him dead, I tugged on

John's coat. "I really am feeling bad," I said. John just laughed. Living on the edge had always attracted John.

We were all sitting in Terpil's study as he chatted on the phone with a fellow gunrunner. Beautiful Cyra sat on the edge of the desk with one leg perched on Terpil's chair. She opened a drawer and pulled out a gun at least a foot long. Just then, Terpil's teenage son appeared to tell Frank, "They're watching the house again, dad."

I could just see myself caught in the crossfire as whoever "they" were burst in the door.

I got up from the couch and lay down on the floor, explaining to everyone that only lying on the floor gets rid of my chronic headaches. I had never had a headache in my life, but I figured that the floor was the safest place in the room.

Terpil invited us to stay for dinner, but I once again mentioned how terrible I was feeling. Cyra walked with me to the car. She said, "Let me show you the present Frank bought me." We went to her black Fiat, and she opened the door and reached into the glove compartment and produced a small, pearl-handled gun. "How lovely," I said. I couldn't get to our car fast enough.

Before we left, Terpil asked John if he could help Cyra get her passport. John, the perpetual politician, said, "Of course. Rita will drive her down tomorrow. Won't you, Rita?"

I agreed. I had no choice.

John's trial began as scheduled the first week in September. Frank Terpil skipped his bail and fled the country that same week.

The jury process was slow. The hours of listening to videotapes and government witnesses seemed endless.

Now and then, unwittingly or otherwise, I became the center of attention.

At one point, the prosecution accused me of talking to some of the jurors. Judge Penn asked me to stand up, and then he asked the potential jurors if I had approached them. They said, "No."

Then there was the day I gave Mel Weinberg (one of the FBI agents who had posed as John Stowe's "financial people") the body-language version of a four-letter put-down. This incident made headlines.

Judge Penn, on one occasion, stated that I was making faces at Reid Weingarten, one of the prosecuting attorneys and that I should stop doing this or be banned from the courtroom. (I had already been banned from hearing the prosecution witnesses because I was a defense witness and had spent two weeks roaming the halls and having confrontations with various FBI personnel.) John's lawyer, Benny Robinson, told the judge that Weingarten was glaring at me. Judge Penn joked that he had noticed Weingarten glaring at him, too.

Just facing each day became more and more unbearable. Each morning, John Miles, John's administrative assistant, would drive us to the courthouse. We developed a kind of ritual out of the journey. We would drive through the Capitol grounds, wave at the Capitol Hill policemen and a stray congressman or two, and then take a left at the Russell Senate Office Building heading up Independence Avenue toward the U.S. District Courthouse.

As we neared the entrance to the courthouse, the ever-waiting newsmen would scramble trying to figure out which entrance we would choose. I would say, "Here we go again." John would straighten his tie. John Miles would sigh, and we'd bolt from the car.

The press would surround John and me as we

pushed toward the entrance. They were aggressive but, on the whole, polite. In fact, John and I developed a warm rapport with the reporters assigned to the trial. They soon became our only friendly refuge in an otherwise hostile environment.

The trial droned on and on. I felt hopeful whenever our close friends would drop by, but always in the back of my mind I knew the jury of John's peers would convict him.

The videotapes were damning. I must say, the evening John and I viewed the tapes I was more than distraught. I sat there, seeing a strange new side of my husband. "I have larceny in my blood," John said on tape.

And John Stowe laughingly told Mel Weinberg, "John is the only man I know who goes after a piece on the way to have a piece." Then he and Weinberg and DeVito laughed.

I thought, *How could John have been so stupid? A child could have seen through this setup.* They always ushered John to the same seat and even had Stowe move one time when he sat in John's seat, which was squarely in front of the hidden camera. DeVito and Weinberg would ask John to repeat things in such an obvious way!

During the trial, John Stowe's wife, Barbara, and I became friends. She told me she was probably going to divorce him. (Subsequently, she did.) She said, "I can't believe our husbands were taken in by that piece of shit" as she glared down the hall at Mel Weinberg. As Barbara and I passed Weinberg, he snickered at us. I whirled on the ball of my foot and "gave him the finger." I had been warned by Judge John Garrett Penn not to talk to him, but the judge didn't say that I couldn't gesture.

Lee Bandy, a close friend of mine and reporter for *The State* newspaper (Columbia, South Carolina), told me later that day that he asked if Weinberg was under FBI guard to keep the press away. The FBI agent said, "No. We are protecting him from Rita Jenrette."

Kenny Robinson was a study in theatrics and often brilliant strategy. He struts around the room like a peacock, always pulling up his baggy trousers. He is handsome in an earthy sort of way. He would alternately have the room laughing or in tears. I knew if anyone could get John exonerated, it would be flamboyant Kenny, whose theatrics contrasted sharply with the cool, methodical brilliance of John Kotelly and his fiery-tempered assistant, Reid Weingarten.

Kenny's beautiful, blonde wife Jean is the most important person in his life. She would sit next to me in the front row, and I kept noticing Kenny looking at her for approval and the loving way she would smile back at him.

When Kenny completed his final argument, there was hardly a dry eye in the courtroom.

Mr. Kotelly rose to give his final rebuttal, clearly and logically stating the government's case. I knew we were sunk. As Kotelly spoke, jurors actually nodded in agreement. As Kotelly wound up each point, even I thought, *Well, that makes sense.*

We were prepared for a long wait for the jury's verdict, perhaps overnight. Kenny's secretary had brought sandwiches and sodas. We holed up in Kenny's office. I sat on a hard, wooden bench. John was in the black leather chair facing Kenny. And Kenny was leaning back in his large leather chair with his feet propped up on his well-worn desk. The phone rang. Kenny's feet flew off the desk and hit the ground with a thud as he picked up the receiver. He looked at me, then at John. This was it, then—and the jury had only been out for a little over two hours. I felt somehow suspended in space and time, not really a part of what was happening. I could see Kenny's lips move but could hear only muffled sounds. It seemed as though everyone was gliding in slow motion. In slow motion, I went to John and placed my hand on his shoulder. He got up, wobbly. We hugged each other.

The block between Kenny's office and the courthouse had never seemed longer. John and I silently walked, hand in hand, oblivious to the cars honking, people staring.

I kept thinking, *Why hadn't Kenny played his guitar?* I knew that he had a custom of always playing his guitar and singing Willie Nelson tunes while the jury was out. He said he'd never lost a case when he played his guitar. He hadn't played his guitar today.

We moved heavily past the media troops and up the steps, through security and onto the elevators. We never stopped holding hands, but we never, during that long walk, looked at each other.

I was aware of reporters milling around us as we made our way to the door of the courtroom where John squeezed my hand, then absent-mindedly kissed my lips before he pushed open the two wooden swinging doors and took his seat at the defense table.

John Kotelly and Reid Weingarten nervously fidgeted with their files, which lay on the table in front of them. Kotelly and Weingarten were a study in contrasts—Kotelly, the Ivy League button-down type, and Weingarten, fiery and brash with that untamed, curly head of hair.

Judge Penn nodded to the tall silver-haired foreman to bring in the twelve jurors who would change the course of our lives. One by one, they slowly filed in, none of them looking in John's direction. The foreman, an attractive black woman, stood. As Judge Penn called out each charge against John, she responded, "Guilty." "Guilty." "Guilty."

John lowered his head and wept, then sobbed. I sat on the edge of the front pew and grasped the seat with both hands as though I might slip off. I didn't cry. I was numb.

A young black woman on the jury was crying softly as she confirmed the guilty verdict. She couldn't look at John. Her head was lowered, so that her voice had an eery quality.

Another juror, a tall, thin, elderly man who was a retired carpenter, kept looking at John sadly over the rims of his glasses. John's father had been a carpenter.

The entire jury seemed relieved to be going home after six long weeks of being sequestered. Their ordeal was over. Ours was beginning. Again.

I reflected on the irony of the situation. John had eight years ago defeated John L. McMillan, an ardent segregationist and chairman of the District of Columbia committee. McMillan had kept the District of Columbia from obtaining home rule with representation in Congress. McMillan had been in office for thirty-three years when John defeated him. John's victory paved the way for home rule in D.C. and two years later placed John in a position to bring representation to the poor, the black, the elderly, to people who had never had someone to look out for them. Yet the twelve jurors, ten of whom were black, had found John Jenrette guilty.

John pulled himself up as though he had tremendous weights attached to his body. He shuffled, sobbing, to the place where I was sitting. I stood up, and although the wooden gate separated us, we half clung to each other, his arms around my waist and my arms around his neck. He went limp in my arms, and I led him to the opening in the wood rail. I could barely move under his weight. He couldn't stop crying. I had to be strong.

The news people ignored our obvious need for a moment alone. Kenny guided us toward the stairs, and we slowly descended them together. When we reached the ground floor, we walked over to a pay phone, and I called John's children. The line was busy.

John and I held each other there in the courthouse for a long time. "It's all right," I told him. "The trial is over. At least we have each other. That's all that matters in the world, anyway. Being a congressman is not important. The only important thing is how we treat those people we love the most."

We finally made our way down the corridor with newsmen trailing us the entire way. As we approached the front door, I could see the icy network lights against the darkness outside. We both took deep breaths and descended the three steps, through the glass door and out into the waiting crowd. The questions came at us. John cried. I cried. Then a reporter asked John if he had any idea what his constituents might think of him now. I angrily turned and glared into the camera. "Who cares what they think?" I said.

People still ask me today how I could have thought John was innocent after seeing the tapes at the trial, after hearing a jury of his peers find him guilty. Well, the answer to that is the same as the answer to people who want to know why I still believed he was faithful even after seeing him in the arms of another woman: I loved John. I loved him, and I grew up believing that if you're married to a man you love, you stay next to him no matter what, in sickness and in health, for better or for worse.

This was for worse, certainly, but I thought that this is why we were married: he needed a woman to believe him when no one else did.

And no one else did. Except me.

John spent the next few days in bed, unable to talk, unable to eat, unable to contemplate going on with his life. He took Dalmane and tried to sleep his sorrow away. I handled all his calls and letters. I dealt with staff requests and made decisions that had to be made.

I felt that John should resign rather than risk expulsion by his colleagues. I didn't see how he could win his general election less than a month away.

We seriously discussed the possibility of my running for his seat. John decided that if he didn't run, then I was the only other person he could support.

Governor Richard W. Riley was adamantly opposed to my taking John's place on the ballot. He felt that a woman couldn't win.

And it soon became clear that John was beginning to regain his old political spirit. He wasn't about to give his congressional seat away to a Thurmond-backed, thirty-three-year-old novice. No, sir. He'd fight to the death.

So instead of the much-needed vacation we thought we'd take in the aftermath of the trial, John and I found ourselves thrown into a desperately underfinanced campaign. We were all over the Sixth Congressional district, meeting plant gates, shaking hands, attending dinners, debating and handing out Redskin footballs to high schools. I sensed early on that we just couldn't win. Yes, John still had a hard core of support, and you could feel it picking up every day. But there just wasn't enough time.

I don't think any human being could have done as well as John did. He came within four-thousand votes of winning. His own home area of Myrtle Beach defeated him. He was astounded and deeply saddened by this.

I was also astounded but not by his loss. What shocked me was how he could have expected anything else under the circumstances. John had always felt invincible. Now he simply had to face it: he had failed.

NBC had predicted that John would win. We had been jubilant as we sat with John's staff in the cramped room at Horne's Motel.

Then our happiness turned to disbelief as Napier began gaining in John's own home county. Within an hour, by eleven P.M., we knew it was over— everyone knew, that is, but John.

John became angry with me when I suggested that he concede. Finally, as we left Horne's to drive to the Quality Inn to greet five hundred of John's supporters, I convinced John that he must concede to Napier. With great reluctance, he agreed.

We made our way to the old post office where the Napier celebrants had gathered.

John Napier and his wife, Pam, kissed me. Napier tried to shake John's hand. John refused. I was shocked by his rudeness.

Napier had made a friendly overture to John in front of the crowd. Instead of conceding the election, John said he'd wait and see what the votes tallied up to the next day. It was too close to call, he said. Some Napier supporters booed; others were too drunk to react.

John quickly left the stage as Napier again tried to shake his hand. I said my good-bys to the Napier's, and I could see that John Napier felt sorry for John. As we departed, I saw a member of the Napier staff hand a bouquet of roses to Pam. I thought that in six years John's staff never made such a kind gesture toward me. I thought *God bless you, Pam. You don't know what you're getting into.*

But my sorrow quickly changed to a feeling of relief as I realized that a great weight had been lifted from my shoulders now that the torch had passed.

The next stop was the Quality Inn, where five hundred Jenrette supporters had held their vigil. John was silent during the drive. As we pulled up into the curved drive of the Quality Inn, John's supporters surrounded the car. We got out of the car. People were touching and kissing us, crying for this man they idolized, the man who had made them feel so very special. John, when he wanted to, could always make a person feel special.

We waded through the mass of well-wishers; as usual, I clung to John's arm, trying not to be swept aside as I had so many times before. It was no mean feat this time. People were frenzied, weeping, many of them trying to cling to John as hard as I was.

John made a tearful address to these people. His composure was gone. The emotion of the evening— no, the emotions of the entire, dreadful year—enveloped the room. The promising young political star who had held so much hope for those who had no hope shone brighter than ever for one brief moment. And then the light was out.

The knowledge that John had brought this tragedy on himself made it no easier to bear. I think John at last was absorbing the impact of what he had done to himself.

Seven

Going Public

The question I am most often asked by reporters is "Why are you so eager for publicity?"

And my stock answer is: "I don't look for publicity. It finds me."

John and I, after all, made the pages of *People* magazine in the early stages of our romance because our jobs didn't jibe. And, it seems, once you've attained that kind of notoriety, you're forever under scrutiny by reporters or gossip columnists looking for juicy tidbits to throw to their readers. This is not only the American way; the paparazzi in Italy, for instance, are even more persistent than they are here. The news media and the public have worked together to create a species of people who exist apart from everyone else, whom other people watch and talk about—celebrities. It doesn't matter what a celebrity does for a living or how well he or she does it. And the attention the celebrity receives, or the money, is often undeserved in ordinary terms, such as how hard that person works or how good or smart he or she is.

I joined, by accident, the ranks of celebrities and peripherally and perhaps briefly, this has made me awfully defensive because I know who I am and what my life has been like and what I've done. When I see the media distortions of me and my life, I want to say, "Hey, stop, you've got me all wrong." I want to explain, set the record straight.

So the headlines read "Tell-All Rita." And perhaps I have talked and told too much to the press, creating the impression that I'm a publicity seeker.

The truth is, my candor during Abscam was to attempt to clear my husband, not to get publicity for myself. As for my alleged press baiting since then—my revelations about my married life in articles in the *Washington Post* and *Playboy*—I wanted people to know that being a congressional wife wasn't all champagne and ticker-tape parades.

It was while reading over my diaries one day not long after John lost the election that I got the idea of writing something about myself. It occurred to me that my experiences might interest other women, not just those who are immersed, through marriage, in the Washington scene but women in general, especially those who have experienced or are experiencing or might one day go through loss of selfhood through what is supposed to be the greatest thing that can happen in life—falling in love. I had read *The Women's Room* and shuddered at the extent to which I identified with the heroine, although I was years younger and therefore a member of the first generation to grow up "liberated"—supposedly. I wondered how many other women my age and even younger were falling into the same trap I did, the martyred-by-marriage trap that Marilyn French so chillingly delineates in *The Women's Room*.

I thought about going public. For the first time in a long time, I had a surge of feeling as if my life, apart from my husband's, was worth something. As a congressman's wife or as the wife of the particular congressman I married, I hadn't been able to do as much as I would have liked in the way of social and cultural programs. Well, I could still contribute something of value—and not just to the Sixth District of South Carolina—an honest account of what I'd just lived through. I felt exhilarated at the thought. I also felt frightened and a bit presumptuous. Maybe I didn't have anything worthwhile to say, after all. Maybe, like me, all the other women I was foolish enough to dream of helping have to learn through their own mistakes. After all, I had been warned. And I certainly hadn't listened.

Something happens when you fall in love. It's matter over mind. The phenomenon is as old as human life. "The heart has reasons," wrote the seventeenth-century French philosopher Blaise Pascal, "that reason cannot understand." Psychiatrists are unable to explain fully the lengths to which people go to protect and preserve relationships that, to outsiders, might seem nightmarish. If I tried to explain love and what it does to you, then I'd really be presumptuous!

I sat thinking all this over, my diaries in my lap, for a long time. Then I called two close friends, Kathy and Rudy Maxa. Although Rudy is the gossip columnist for the *Washington Post,* he was—and is—one of the few people in Washington I trust totally. He and Kathy were immediately enthusiastic about the idea of my coauthoring with Kathy an article about what it was really like to be married to a powerful political figure. We began work right away. Whenever Kathy and I became discouraged, Rudy was right there to spur us on. When the article proposal was finished, Kathy submitted it to *McCall's* where the feeling was that the subject matter, in addition to being a little too steamy for *McCall's,* was probably of interest only to residents of the District of Columbia. It was too parochial for a national magazine.

Kathy called me in South Carolina. She said she wanted to sell the story to the *Washington Post Magazine* or to the *Washingtonian* magazine. I said, "Go ahead." We both were a bit down about *McCall's* lukewarm reception.

"Diary of a Mad Congresswife" appeared as the cover story in the *Washington Post Magazine* on December 7, 1980—Pearl Harbor Day! I suppose I should have seen this as some kind of omen. Looking back, I guess it was. Kathy and I, for all our belief that we had an intriguing story to tell, never anticipated the national attention the article received. The story was syndicated in several newspapers, including the *American Statesman* in my home town, Austin, Texas. The resulting furor was unbelievable. Reaction in New York surfaced on page one headlines in the *New York Post*.

Calls requesting my presence on TV and radio talk shows flooded in from across the country. I received bushels of mail, some admiring, other letters expressing absolute hatred, a brand of rancor I had never experienced. I simply could not believe that telling the truth could elicit such a deluge of emotions from total strangers.

The response was particularly—and, I suppose, predictably, had I bothered to make any predictions—vitriolic in South Carolina. In Myrtle Beach, they came up with a song, "Ode to Rita," an anything-but-flattering ditty that went like this: "You think you're so pretty and you think you've got so much class/But Rita, you ain't nothin' but a pain in the ———"

Actually, the tune is rather catchy. But I know all too well it was the lyrics that made the records sell like chicken bog at a Myrtle Beach church benefit. Throughout South Carolina, cars started sporting bumper stickers that said, "John and Rita Who?" Posters and T-shirts with a caricature of me popped up overnight. Radio shows held contests: "Who will Rita name next?" I had become the woman that at least half the state loved to hate.

John's relatives wasted no time in letting me know their feelings. They sent rude, distasteful letters, one woman saying she was hiring a lawyer to force me to stop using the name Jenrette.

Beyond South Carolina, the crazies came out of the woodwork and were attacking me with a vengeance. There were quite a few articles depicting me as a publicity-grubbing femme fatale. Or just your standard steretype woman with a big mouth. Mike Royko, a syndicated columnist, called me "the most terrifying woman he had ever seen." I won't attempt to describe his column or tell you what I think of it. You decide what *you* think of it:

> If you just look at the bare facts, it's not easy to feel sorry for someone like John Jenrette, Jr., the disgraced former Congressman from South Carolina. He has been convicted in the Abscam bribe case. He was a lush, a skirt-chaser. He had to slink out of Congress before being thrown out.
>
> But, holy cow, should even a crooked politician—even a dog—have to endure what Jenrette is being subjected to?
>
> I am talking about his wife, Rita, the new star of the press, TV talk shows and *People* magazine and one of the most terrifying women I've ever seen.
>
> By now most people know their story . . .

Suddenly it was all over the front pages: Rita mercilessly detailing her husband's extra-marital indiscretions.

This is the kind of stuff that sometimes oozes out of divorce hearings. But amazingly, Rita did her blabbing while she and Jenrette were still together and planned to remain together. Rita said it was just something she had to get off her ample chest . . .

. . . Under our system of law, we forbid cruel and unusual punishments. No floggings, tearing out fingernails, walking on hot coals, or other tortures.

There are even agencies, public and private, to protect animals from mistreatment.

But there is nothing to protect someone like Jenrette from the terrors of Rita. There is no Anti-Cruelty society for wimps.

John Jenrette is just the latest male victim of the alarming tendency among many modern women to tell all.

Actresses now give interviews and write books about all the famous men they have slept with. Men don't do such unchivalrous things. You don't see men writing books about the women they slept with. Men don't give interviews ridiculing their former girlfriends. Men don't go telling their wives' secrets to the newspapers.

I don't know why women are acting this way, but I have some advice for them. Ladies, please try to act like gentlemen.

It was not my idea to pose for *Playboy*. That notion originated with the gentleman to whom I was married. He had just given a press conference and announced that he wouldn't resign from Congress;

he would fight to remain a congressman. Among the people in our home following the press conference were Peter Ross Range, *Playboy*'s editor in Washington. At the time, *Playboy* had expressed interest in Kathy and me writing an article for the magazine, elaborating on *Diary of a Mad Congresswife*. John said to Peter, "Why don't you use Rita as a centerfold?"

"Oh, that's ridiculous," I said.

Peter smiled. The subject was dropped—for the time being.

My decision to acquiesce was a matter of economics. John needed money to pay for his legal fees. *Playboy* would pay Kathy and me well for the article, I was told; but they would pay much more for an article accompanied by a pictorial.

Whatever I was paid, I was splitting it fifty-fifty with Kathy. So I wanted to earn as much as possible.

As it turned out, I never got to contribute to John's legal fees because we separated.

But there was another reason for posing for *Playboy*. It was ultimately a kind of reaffirmation of myself, of the self that had been submerged and even lost during my marriage to John. It was proof to myself—not to the world but to *me*—that I am a complete person, able to do what I want, married or not married. To some people, I know, the idea of disrobing, even partially, in a photographer's studio and then permitting the photos to be published is indiscreet, immodest, indecent, even scandalous. For me it was out of character but something I had to do to prove a point: that I am a person in my own right.

I remember that after I went to Chicago to do the test shooting, I brought some Polaroids home with me and showed them to John. He examined them in silence, then said, "Why don't you forget the photos and just do the story?" I wondered if he had forgotten that he had been the one to initiate the idea of my posing seminude in the first place. But I didn't say anything. That evening, he took a verbal stab at my new-found confidence: "Why would they want a thirty-one-year-old woman in their magazine?" he wanted to know. The remark hurt me; it also helped me make up my mind to go ahead with the shooting.

The Los Angeles segment of the *Playboy* shooting went smoothly. The professionalism of photographer Pompeo Posar and the rest of the staff rubbed off on me. I had stopped being nervous and was working hard and enjoying myself—until John showed up. The reason that he had not come to California with me in the first place was that the Ethics Committee was meeting to decide whether he should be expelled from Congress. On the night before the *Playboy* photography began, I had heard that the Ethics Committee had recommended John's expulsion and that he had resigned. I was shocked. My husband had resigned from Congress and he hadn't even bothered to inform me. He had the phone numbers where I could be reached. But I had to hear the news from a TV anchorman.

I immediately called one of John's secretaries, who told me that she had driven him to the airport and he was going to New York. I was incredulous. "Why New York?" Nobody knew.

John arrived at my hotel in L.A. at around three A.M. He said that he had been on the Tom Snyder show that night—his reason for going to New York. The following day, he came to the photography session with me. He bounded through the studio, shaking hands with everyone, greeting them in his booming politician's voice, "Hi! I'm John Jenrette!" He seemed to be trying to steal my show, as if he couldn't stand his wife being the center of attention instead of him. I had begun to feel sorry for him. The resignation must have been so difficult, suddenly finding himself stripped of the position he had worked so hard to attain. But then John interrupted the photo session. He picked up one of the Polaroids, looked at it, and said, "Ugh." My sympathy quickly turned to hurt, then anger.

Christmas of that year was a bleak time. John and I went to my parents' home in Austin, Texas, with John's son, Hal, with whom, after a rocky start, I had developed a warm relationship. He seemed now to respond to me not merely as his stepmother, whom he had to accept one way or another, but as a friend. That Christmas, I truly appreciated being with Hal and, of course, with my parents, who had not quite recovered from the shock of hearing that their little girl had bared her soul— among other things—in *Playboy*. But my mother and dad do have faith in my judgment; I think they had more or less decided to postpone their hysteria until they actually saw whether or not the pictures warranted it. "Well, as long as you didn't actually take off *all* your clothes," my mother sighed occasionally.

Both my parents tried hard to make Christmas as lovely and peaceful as it's supposed to be, as it always was when I was a child. The tree was bright and beautiful; my favorite ornament, a little porcelain angel, was on the mantel as it always had been. On Christmas day, my parents surprised me with some beautiful shirts and makeup as well as some money. They knew that the money would come in handy.

At this point, I was John's sole source of income. We had astronomical legal fees. The house mortgage, the car payments, the insurance, all fell on my shoulders. This financial pressure further eroded John's low self-esteem following his retirement from Congress; I had tried to buoy his low spirits and build his confidence by consulting him about my career plans—ideas, the songs I was writing— but instead of responding with any sort of enthusiasm, he would always be negative, disillusioning. Over the Christmas holidays, I struggled continually to keep John's depression, which was more than justifiable under the circumstances, from dampening everyone's mood.

It seemed illogical to me that John should be so unsupportive of my career plans in light of the fact that I was paying almost all our bills! There was no point in his trying to undermine my opportunities to earn money, such as the TV film deal brewing in Los Angeles. A producer wanted the rights to my story. But he needed a release form signed by John. Because of a major lawsuit that CBS had just settled over a docudrama, all networks were requiring iron-clad release forms from people who would be portrayed in TV movies. The producer sent a release form to Austin for John to sign. And John refused to sign.

I was exasperated. The money for the movie could be used to pay for his appeal! John's lawyer was constantly asking us for the money we owed him already. But John was convinced that the movie would depict him in a negative light. (In fact, the plans were to portray him very sympathetically.) There was no reasoning with him. Finally, however, he prepared a watered-down version of the release and signed it.

On January 2, John and I left Austin, going, as usual, in two different directions. I headed for L.A. to appear on the John Davidson show and to continue negotiations on the movie deal. John flew to Washington. He told me he was going to seclude himself in our house. He needed time to be totally alone, to relax. For five days, I called John, mostly early in the morning and late at night when I was sure he would be in. There was never an answer. Had John still been drinking heavily, I would have suspected him of being with another woman—or women. But John had been sober for ten months. I was worried sick. Maybe he had taken his own life. I called Rudy and Kathy Maxa and asked them to go over to our house. Seconds after I hung up the receiver, the phone rang. "Hi, Rita!" John drawled.

"John! Where have you been for the last five days?"

"Why, Miami!"

My worry and the subsequent relief at hearing the familiar Southern twang disappeared abruptly. "Frankly, John," I said, "if you had said you'd been in Tahiti, I couldn't have been more surprised."

"Well," he said, "I didn't want to stay in Washington during the swearing in of the new members of Congress."

We made plans to meet the next day in Chicago to go on the "Jay Levine Show" together. John left me two messages the next day. The first one said that he would arrive in Chicago at seven P.M. The second revised his arrival time to nine P.M. He showed up at one A.M. His plane, he explained, had been delayed. As he reached over to kiss me, I got a whiff of musk perfume. "John," I said, "you ought to tell your girl friends never to wear musk oil. It carries from the woman to the man." I was surprised at my calmness. In earlier years, I was so hurt whenever I suspected John of being unfaithful. But by now I was indifferent. I was changing. If he had been with a woman in Miami, so what?

We sat on the couch in the luxurious suite provided by ABC in Chicago. ABC had gone to the trouble of sending up Godiva chocolates, cheese, fruits, and an ample supply of my beloved Diet Dr. Peppers. I sipped one of the sodas, and John sampled the chocolates as we talked—or as I tried to maintain a conversation. As usual, I was trying to convey my feelings to John, and he was exercising his politician's gift of avoiding any issue he doesn't want to discuss.

I told him that I realized now, for the first time, how empty I felt when I was with him and how angry I was at him. "I'm angry about the humiliating way in which you've flaunted your affairs," I said. "In fact, I think you wanted everyone to know about your indiscretions. Before we got married, I told you that if you can't be monogamous, at least be discreet so I'll never know about it. But it really seems as if you not only wanted me to know but everyone else in the world. So now you were in Miami. And I assumed you were with your old flame the Eastern Airlines stewardess."

"I haven't seen Cindy in ten years. We've talked on the phone a couple times, but I swear to you I haven't seen her. You're just being jealous again—and Cindy is one old girl friend I wouldn't hesitate for you to meet."

When John told me that night that he wouldn't be accompanying me back to Washington after our talk-show appearance—he wanted to go to Miami again to "rest up" a bit more—I was actually relieved. I, too, needed to "rest up"—from my relationship with John.

The "Jay Levine Show" was a good experience. I got some much-needed practice in fielding tough questions. Mr. Levine was extremely well prepared. During the course of the interview, he asked John his reaction to my forthcoming *Playboy* article and photos. John said, "I will be very shocked if Rita posed for *Playboy*." I nearly fell out of my chair! Fortunately, I remembered that TV cameras were rolling. For once, I kept my mouth shut. But I was furious. After all, hadn't John actually visited the *Playboy* set in L.A.? Hadn't he enjoyed the hospitality at Hefner's mansion just as much as I did? The only reason for his alleged, anticipated "shock" must have been that he was still playing the politician, thinking about his image in the eyes of his constituents.

On our way back to the hotel, John told me that his cousin, Dick Jenrette, president of the Donaldson Lufkin and Jenrette Inc. stock brokerage in New York City, was upset with my revelations in the *Washington Post* article. John, however, had rushed to my defense. It took all of his persuasive powers, John said, to talk Dick into continuing to handle the money I had had his firm invest for me.

When we reached the hotel, I immediately called my broker at Donaldson Lufkin and Jenrette Inc. and told him what John had said. My broker checked John's story with Dick, who denied ever having had such a discussion with John.

I wondered why John was trying to convince me that people disliked me because of the *Post* article. I supposed that his insecurities had reached an all-time high.

In the limousine going to the airport, John kept asking me what was wrong. I couldn't even respond.

That evening, back in Washington, I found our blue Mercedes in the congressional parking area at National Airport and slowly drove through the freezing rain to our home. As I passed the Capitol, it looked unreal, like a picture. I knew we had been severed forever from this town, this life-style, the personae we had become here.

Almost as soon as I walked in the door of our house, the phone rang. It was a friend of ours from Myrtle Beach, South Carolina. He started raking me over the coals for having written so descriptively about the Sixth District in my *Post* article. He said it was rumored that John and I were divorcing. I said, "That's news to me." Then he asked me whether I knew, at that moment, where John was and who he was with. His implication was obvious.

I thought, *I'll be damned if I'm going to stand by John anymore if he's going to continue to deceive me.* When he drank, I always rationalized his behavior. But he was sober now.

I called the Florida telephone number John had given me. It was bogus. So was the address of the place where he was supposedly staying.

I called John Moran, the friend of ours who, according to John, had rented the condominium for John's Miami visit. Moran said, "Gee, I'm sorry, but I don't know the number."

"Listen," I said, "I've been lied to for five years now. John lied to me. His staff and his friends lied to me. And I don't have room or time in my life anymore for people who lie to me. So if you're lying, just write me off as a friend. And I've been a good friend to you—better than John has—and you know it."

"Okay," Moran said. "I was lying. John called me last Sunday and said 'I am going down to visit an old girl friend in Miami. It's completely innocent, but Rita wouldn't understand. So if Rita calls you, please cover for me.'"

Moran went on to tell me that he thought John was acting irrationally, deceiving me after all we had been through and on top of that, asking a friend of mine to aid in the coverup.

My next phone call that night was to Rudy and Kathy Maxa. I told Kathy, "Tell the *Playboy* people that I'm sorry, and if it ruins their piece, I can't help it, but I am leaving John. I'm divorcing him." I then recounted the Miami saga to Rudy. Rudy listened quietly, then asked me how John, who was broke, was financing his stay in Miami. I told Rudy that I had seen John take money from his closet not long ago. He had explained to me that the cash— $100 bills—was for our living expenses; he had stashed it away and didn't tell me about it because he was angry with me for having bought my parents furniture for Christmas—an extravagance, he thought.

Rudy asked me, "How do you know he's telling you the truth about the money?"

"I don't know," I said. "I don't know anything anymore."

Rudy then suggested that I look through John's closet.

After we ended our conversation, I walked upstairs, feeling utterly drained. I got into bed and lay there, watching Ted Koppel on "ABC's Night Line." But I couldn't stop wondering about the possible contents of John's closet. Finally, overcome with curiosity, I got out of bed and opened the closet door. I immediately noticed the white athletic sock half stuffed into one of John's brown suede shoes. This was odd. John is unusually neat; he wouldn't leave a sock lying there like that. I picked up the sock. There was a red bag stuffed in the shoe. In the bag was more cash than I had ever seen in one place in my life. I counted the money: $25,000, in mostly $100 bills.

I was terrified. If this was Abscam money—and where else would John have gotten it?—I had been defending a guilty man. If I now tried to protect

John, would I be guilty, too? Would I go to jail? Should I call a lawyer? Will the FBI think I knew about the money all along? What should I do? Who should I call? If only John hadn't given me a bogus phone number. Oh, God, why did I look in that closet in the first place?

I called Rudy. He may be a reporter, I reasoned, but he's first and foremost my friend. He told me to come and spend the night with him and Kathy. I picked up the red bag containing the money, my purse, my coat, and jumped in the car, leaving every light on in the house.

As I started the car, I noticed the gas gauge was on empty. Where would I find a gas station that was open at this hour of the night? Here I was with $25,000, driving around Capitol Hill, which is not the world's safest place, and about to run out of gas. In front of the Capitol building, I stopped to ask two policemen where the nearest gas station was. They told me there was a station a few blocks away. Then the younger of the two said, "You're Mrs. Jenrette, aren't you?"

"Yes," I said.

"We really want you to know we admire you and what you're doing. People should know what we employees here at the Hill see year in and year out. Everything you've said is true—and more."

This was a scene from a movie, I thought, not my life. There I sat, listening to two policemen praising my integrity, and I had this $25,000 of mysterious origins on the seat next to me!

Kathy Maxa was wearing a nightgown and robe when she opened her door for me at 2:30 A.M. Rudy took my purse and coat and led me to the couch. We talked; I cried for about an hour. The mood was funereal; none of us laughed or smiled. I felt as if someone had just died; in fact part of me had.

At noon the next day, my lawyer, Jim Abourezk, came by. I told him that I didn't want to hurt John. But I wanted to do whatever was right—and legal.

Jim agreed with me He said, "We'll put the money in a safe deposit box at the Riggs Bank, and we'll try to find John and get an explanation from him. If it is untainted money, fine. No one will ever know. If it's not, you will and must turn it over to the FBI."

Now began the four-day process of trying to track down John. I searched the house for his ex-girl friend's phone number. Rudy used his Miami criss-cross directory. We came up empty. Finally, on Sunday, right after the Super Bowl game, John called our house. Rudy, who was there with Kathy helping me pack John's things, answered the phone. He asked John about the money, and John said it came from treasury bills and from money he had hidden during his first divorce.

Rudy asked John why he had lied to me about his whereabouts. John responded, "Sure I lied. I'm down here in Miami with an old girl friend and her fiancé. Rita just wouldn't understand. She got all upset in Chicago."

While this was taking place, Kathy and I were packing John's clothes in boxes. I wanted this man out of my life. I had made up my mind. I refused to stand by my man if he refused to stand by me. That's how I felt, then, for the first time in my life, and it's how I feel today. Marriage is a two-way street. John is, I'm afraid, a one-way man.

As I was folding up a blue corduroy suit, the jacket fell open, and I saw a bulge in the inside pocket. I reached inside and found $1,700 in $100 bills held together by a rubber band. Kathy, Rudy and I just stared at each other. I asked Rudy to put the money in the safe deposit box. He placed the

$1,700 on top of the $25,000 already in the box. (This would prove significant later.)

The week that followed was the most upsetting and confusing of my life. As I lay in bed every night, fear swept over me. I was really alone now. But the die was cast. There was no way to turn back the clock and pretend that the events of the past week hadn't happened, especially since the press now was in on the secret. It's my opinion that John's lawyer, Kenny Robinson, leaked the news to a wire service that I had found the money in John's shoe. Later, Kenny would tell reporters that I had let the story out, but I had been completely quiet about it. So had my lawyer. And it was only after Rudy Maxa saw the story that he wrote his own piece for the *Washington Post*.

Then some close friends in Myrtle Beach called several reporters in South Carolina to inform them that I was divorcing John. I had confided in them, hoping that they might know where John was staying in Miami.

John flew back to Washington. A flock of reporters awaited him at the airport.

On national TV, John, with tears in his eyes, told Fred Graham that his mother left him part of the $25,000 and that the rest was given to him as Christmas gifts.

I was staying at the Maxas. I couldn't bring myself to watch John on television. I knew that despite all that had happened to me during my marriage to John Jenrette, despite my determination to divorce him, he still had a powerful hold on me. I had made up my mind to be strong, but I was afraid that my emotions might propel me into rushing back to him.

Several days after John's return to Washington, he called Kathy Maxa and said that he had injured his eye and needed the Blue Cross/Blue Shield number from me. Kathy phoned him back and gave him the number.

The following morning, John called again. I reluctantly agreed to talk to him. He was crying. He said he would have to be hospitalized. I rushed to the pharmacy for medicine, and Kathy accompanied me to the house. I climbed those familiar stairs, my hand trailing on the beautiful wood bannister, feeling anything but at home. I cautiously rounded the corner outside our bedroom and opened the door. The bedroom was completely dark. The shades were drawn. I turned on the light by the bed. There was John with a patch over his left eye.

He began to cry. But when I touched his face, it was dry. He said, "You've ruined our lives. How could you hurt me so?"

"I'm sorry you feel badly," I said.

"I'm dying. Dr. Carey wants me hospitalized."

"John, I've scratched my cornea a few times. All you have to do is wait a day and it'll heal itself. I know it's painful, but tomorrow you'll be fine. Here. Take these pills I brought you."

He grabbed me. "I love you so much," he said, kissing me passionately and pulling me on to the bed. "I know you want to make love," he said. He was holding me down. I struggled to get away, although part of me didn't want to. Then Kathy, who was still downstairs, called my name. John immediately let me go. "Oh," he said, "so you brought your protector along. Don't you know she's using you?"

I ran to the closet and grabbed a suitcase and started throwing together some of my clothes that I had left behind and my jewelry box—it was only later that I discovered that John had taken the diamond ring my dad had given me when I graduated from college. Every step I took, John followed me, trying to embrace and kiss me. He said, "Come back tonight alone and don't tell Kathy, Rudy, your lawyer not anyone."

I said, "I'll think about it." But I knew I never would do that. I just wanted to get away from him.

He walked with me to the back door and whispered, "Come back tonight. With ten thousand dollars." He was all smiles, so confident that he had won me back.

In the car, I told Kathy what had happened and that if she hadn't been there I don't know what else would have gone on.

I also told my lawyer what had occurred. He said, "John's a lawyer. He knows that if you two had made love it would have negated all that he had done."

I had to get away from John, Washington, and its memories, so I went to New York and literally hid in the apartment of my friends, Bob and Linda, who were in Los Angeles. I stayed in bed for the first few days, getting up only to go to the refrigerator and comfort myself with Diet Dr. Pepper. I felt overwhelmed and immobile. Had I done the right thing? Was John really so bad? Hadn't we had some good times together? As usual, with a few days' and a few miles' distance from him, memories of those good times began edging out the awful, painful memories. I was standing still, incapable of making the least move.

Finally, I began handwriting an agreement, splitting the ownership of the house in Washington, the car, and the stock with John, although everything was in my name. I also stated that he could stay in the house until I rented it or until his hearing on February 10.

When I returned to Washington and showed my lawyer this document, he said, "You're being overly generous." I told him that I just wanted to be fair. John had lost enough.

When I returned to the house to pick up some clothes, I brought some friends with me. But I couldn't get in the door: John had changed the locks! I called a locksmith. After a locksmith let us in, I discovered a few more surprises waiting inside the house. John had taken everything—the antiques, the paintings, the three silk oriental rugs, the china, silver bowls, silver chafing dishes, silver goblets, and the crystal I had brought to our marriage. He stripped the house right down to the microwave oven. He had even removed the chandelier from the dining room ceiling. I immediately called my lawyer and told him, "I don't even have a bed to sleep on."

John did leave me my family heirloom silver flatware. But he took all my other family silver—bowls, chafing dishes, salt and pepper shakers, goblets—and my heirloom crystal decanters. He also left notes numbered one, two, and three taped at various points on the stairway. They were written in very disjointed sentences, messages vacillating from "I love you" to "How could you do this to me?" to "You were going to have me put in jail—" It all seemed so bizarre.

The next day, I moved out the remainder of my clothes, put the house up for rent, and put Washington behind me forever.

I looked out the window of the plane that was taking me to my new home, New York, and stared at the receding terrain of the Capitol where my romance with John had begun and now, sadly, had ended. I knew I would never live in Washington again. I had taken my first small step into a new life-style. I was afraid—but not enough to stay.

I thought that I would not even visit Washington for a long time. But as fate would have it, I had to return the following week to accompany the FBI agents to the Riggs Bank to compare the serial numbers of the money I had found in John's closet with the Abscam money. Ironically, one of the agents was Dave Birch, who had visited our home on February 2, nearly a year ago, to read John his rights.

The agents picked up Jim Abourezk and me. Agent Birch and I exchanged pleasantries. What a change from our previous encounters. I think we were both relieved. "I thought you guys would be driving a Cadillac," I told the agents. "Oh that's right. Only Mel Weinberg ranks a limo." We all laughed. The ice was broken.

The four of us entered the Riggs Bank. People recognized me and their stares were a bit disconcerting.

Jim brought out the safe deposit box, and an officer of the bank showed us to a private room.

Jim and Agent Birch sat on one side of the long conference table and I sat alone on the other side. The second agent sat at the end of the table to my left.

Jim slowly pulled the money out of the red felt bag. Agent Birch opened his black, worn briefcase and handed Jim a copy of the Abscam money serial numbers.

As Jim and Agent Birch perused their lists to check the first $100 bill, I almost lost my composure. I prayed that the numbers would not match. I didn't want John to go to prison. And a part of me, I suppose, wanted to believe that he had not taken the money.

The first bill matched an Abscam serial number. My eyes filled with tears. I covered my face and said, "Oh, no, John, no."

The first thirteen $100 bills matched. But the

remaining $25,000 did not. I suddenly realized that the money had come from the pocket of John's blue corduroy jacket.

The origin of the $25,000 that I found in John's shoe is still a mystery to me.

But what isn't a mystery is I spent five years with a man who spent those five years cheating on me and lying to me. I no longer believe a wife is required to stand by her husband unless he's willing to treat her as he would want to be treated himself. I never lied to or cheated on John. I'm proud of that. I'm not proud of the pain and the punishment I endured, but I will say that it has made me a stronger woman today than I was five years ago.

I'm on my own now. I have no more secrets to share.

Epilogue:
Where Do I Go From Here?

First, let me tell you where "here" is: a hotel room in Washington, D.C. It's midnight, Sunday, March 1, 1981—the end of my first hectic week on the road for *Playboy*, six nearly sleepless nights, and days in front of TV cameras, blinking in the flashbulbs' glare, signing autographs, shaking hands, smiling, and answering question after question. And always a question of my own was on my mind: Why are all these people so interested in me? Don't get me wrong: I love attention as much as the next person. But, frankly, the degree of explosive reaction to my *Playboy* pictorial (did anyone read the article?) was as unexpected as the furor over my *Washington Post* article.

I'm exhausted but exhilarated. I've campaigned for John Jenrette. I've campaigned for Clairol. In a way, I'm now out there selling magazines for *Playboy*—let's face it, this publicity is good for *Playboy*, and I'm happy about it because *Playboy* has been good to me. But, finally, I feel, I'm really campaigning for myself. And that feels good. A lot of reporters have accused me of "capitalizing on John's name," using the fact that I am married to a congressman who was involved in a scandal to launch my own career. One interviewer asked me if

I though I was an "opportunist." As I explained to this interviewer, the word "opportunist" has negative connotations. It means taking advantage of opportunities even though you may have to sacrifice your own principles to do so.

I haven't sacrificed my own principles, but I *am* taking advantage of the media interest in me. But I know that even with this head start, even with the help of the media blitz, surviving as a performer will not be easy. This past week has not been easy. It may look—to reporters, to TV audiences—as if I'm leading a glamorous life, basking in the klieg lights, as if, in short, notoriety is, in itself, rewarding. It's not. It's opening yourself to everyone else's criticism. Even before my tour began, Claudia Cohen wrote some terrible things about me in her "I, Claudia" column in the *Daily News* (New York), saying that she'd heard that I had had a press luncheon at "21", but that she thought I should be at Nedick's.

But the event that everyone knows most about was when John and I had a marital squabble on national TV, on the "Phil Donahue" show. John phoned in, and graciously informed the American public that he wanted his money back.

But John didn't stop at calling Phil Donahue. He phoned me in my hotel suite and said that he was planning to "smear" me by disclosing, with the help of Jack Anderson, that I had had an abortion and that what *Playboy* readers saw in the pictorial was the result of head-to-toe plastic surgery. A friend of John's phoned *Playboy* with similar threats, trying to extort money from the magazine!

I never had an abortion—or plastic surgery. But John did not stop with phone calls. A subpoena was presented to me; I had to appear in court in Washington, D.C. on Monday, March 2, to defend myself since John planned to freeze my money.

It didn't work.

So that is where I am right now. As for where I'm going, I really don't know what the future holds for me. I never could have envisioned the past five years as being as turbulent, as sorrowful, as exuberant, and as fast moving as they have been. I feel as though I've lived fifty years in the last five.

I think I am a survivor. I think I am—but, you know, I've now learned to say, "I think" or "I hope" and never to say "This is definitely the way it will be." I've learned to speak in possibilities, in flexible terms, because I know that although life is finite, there is nothing definite about it.

I hope that my singing career will take off, and that I can do some acting. I hope that the American people can perceive me differently than I've been portrayed by columnists and news reporters out to build their own reputations and audiences. But I've always been misjudged, and maybe I always will be. The important thing is that I can look at myself in the mirror and know that I'm a good and honest person.

And if what I've had to say in this book induces some congressmen to clean up their acts, or saves some congressional wife from hitting the bottle, or otherwise wasting her life, if it somehow helps other women who are married to men who are not politicians, women who are held back or victimized by relationships they are afraid to end, then my "telling all" and the flack I've received as a result will be worth it.

My friends are more important to me than anything now. I'm surrounding myself with really good close warm friends. One of them, Bob Rose, expressed what I'd like to say better than I ever could. "You know" he told me "you've read about movie stars, child stars, who never had a childhood. Well, I think you've never had an adulthood. Oh, you've been exposed to plenty of adultery, but you've never had an adulthood in that Washington playground, among all those children playing with power. Now you're finally free to have wonderful times ahead."

I hope Bob is right.